New Earrings

NEW EARRINGS

500+ CONTEMPORARY JEWELLERY DESIGNS

NICOLAS ESTRADA

HOAKI

HOAKI

Hoaki Books, S.L.
C/ Ausiàs March, 128
08013 Barcelona, Spain
T. 0034 935 952 283
F. 0034 932 654 883
info@hoaki.com
www.hoaki.com

hoakibooks

New Earrings
500 + Contemporary Jewellery Designs

ISBN: 978-84-19220-51-6

© 2024 Hoaki Books, S.L.

Selection of contents and edition: Nicolas Estrada
English translation: Kevin Krell
Layout: spread. David Lorente - Tomoko Sakamoto
Editorial coordination: Anna Tetas Palau
Texts by: © Nicolas Estrada, © Theo Smeets, © Sian Hindle
Cover design: Claudia Martínez Alonso
Cover images: Front: *Ninfa Earcuff* by Valentina Falchi. Photo: © Raúl Mellado.
Back: Images selected from the pages of this book.

D.L: B 4729-2024

Printed in China

Index

This book, then, includes two highly interesting and enjoyable texts, and I am very grateful to Sian and Theo for accepting my invitation and taking the time to write about this subject and our experience with this kind of jewellery.

The book includes more than 500 photographs and a multitude of pieces that will delight the most purist to the most daring and avant-garde earring enthusiast. I very much enjoy the diverse work in which each viewer identifies with a piece, and in this new edition there is jewellery for all tastes. For this reason, I am deeply grateful to all the people who sent me their submission and who, once again, trusted me and accepted my selection criteria.

In conclusion, I again would like to thank Hoaki for their trust in me. As I said before, we have been working together for more than thirteen years now, and they continue to have faith in my passion and choices. I wish to thank, in particular, Anna Tetas for her help with this publication, as well as the entire Hoaki team that participated in its preparation and helped to make the book as exquisite as the jewellery that appears within it. And, of course, thank you, dear reader, for buying the book and making it possible for jewellery to shine and remain in the limelight.

Nicolas Estrada

Respect!

Theo Smeets

As a jewellery maker, I had made about three pairs of earrings so far and at some point decided that they were "not my thing". Somehow, I need to experience the pieces I make on my own body, so there exists at least one piece in my size of every finger ring I have ever made. Also, all my jewellery is regularly examined in front of the mirror during the making process—rings, brooches and necklaces. But earrings? No, I don't wear those—I've tried (with clips) but, man, I find myself looking ridiculous wearing them.... And besides... The piercing—oh my God!

My father was a watchmaker, my parents had a jewellery shop until I was 11. I spent a lot of time there and, as a little boy, I was always fascinated when mothers walked in with their daughters, usually the child of an age when it could not even walk properly. "I want some earrings for my daughter. Mr Smeets," they announced. After the mother had picked out the desired ones for her daughter, my father explained that after the piercing, a so-called "ulcer ring" should be worn for a few weeks to prevent any inflammation. He presented some pairs of such rings and after the mother agreed (who wants their kid to have inflamed ears?), he went to his workbench to sharpen the pins. Back then, in the seventies, there was no such thing as piercing guns—and if there had been, my father would never ever have used them. He had his own method. He came back from his workbench with the earrings, a small piece of cork and some alcohol-soaked cotton wool, sat down on a small stool next to the girl—she was still smiling at him... Carefully he determined the centre of the child's earlobe, and with the cork behind her ear, gently but quickly pushed the sharpened pin through it, dabbed it with alcohol and—and even before her young neuronal system could have passed on any alarm signals to the unsuspecting brain—held out to her a cute, pink-rimmed hand mirror. With the reflection of her new and amazing beauty, the poor thing completely forgot to cry. "How pretty you look with your new earring," my father said to the girl, who then looked at her mother, whose beaming face also clearly stated that everything was perfectly fine! That was when my father grabbed his chance: "Do you want the other one too?" he asked, dangling it under her nose with an innocent smile. Most

'Twelve, love… twelve:
you can have your ears pierced
when you're twelve.'

Sensing Earrings

Sian Hindle

It's an arbitrary number, but twelve is the age when, in my youth, I was told, and—mindful of a kind of familial tradition—this was the age set in our household when my eight year old daughter asked. It varies by country and culture, but this seems to be something of a standard in the UK, capitalising on the holidays prior to starting high school at eleven or twelve to allow ears to heal. For my daughter (and later my son), this adornment signifying autonomy and independence needed to be kept hidden from teachers, particularly those in charge of providing physical education: at this age, ear studs are small, sometimes worn as clear plastic, invisible to the teachers and almost not there at all. The school rules list mitigation for the perceived risks of pierced ears: earrings are tolerated, but must be taped up or taken out for physical activities. This rule might be little-enforced, but the school's desire to control speaks of society's anxiety around children's bodies and the coming-of-age of the young people themselves. This is a taking back of control that I understood myself, at the age of twelve, but it has gained a degree of nuance now that I am a parent. This is a rite of passage that I am a *spectator* to now: a gathering of self that puts reliance on the parent in the shade. The nooks and crannies, bits and slits are theirs (thank goodness) to look after now, but this is a pushing back of the lines of control, and I admire their quiet pride in claiming this space for themselves.

At first, then, earrings are worn silently. Unlike rings or bracelets, which are a visual treat shared between the wearer and the viewer, earrings are worn almost from the inside out. They might be inspected by the wearer's own wandering fingertips, played with unconsciously; felt, but not seen. Studs are barely there, but anything more substantial has a degree of weight and a sense of movement: a shake of the head or movement of the body sets up a rhythm that reminds the wearer of their presence. And then, in its turn, art jewellery takes something more like commitment to wear; the scale, position and materials create a challenge that not everyone is comfortable taking on. Beyond this, because of the foregrounding of the wearer's sense of touch, these adornments require the wearer to *embody* the ideas that are being communicated; but this has a provisional quality. The different sensory experiences of wearer and viewer—one feeling, the other seeing—establishes a kind of dialogue, one that mirrors the conversation that is played out in clothes. Iris Marion Young, in her thought-provoking essay 'Women Recovering Our Clothes', notes, 'as the clothes flow among us, so do our identities; we do not keep hold of ourselves, but share' (Young, 1990: 198).

Ear-piercing sits on the nearside of the line of social acceptability, undertaken—in the UK now, at least—almost as readily by boys and men as women and girls. Whereas piercings elsewhere on the body are performed out of sight, behind a curtain or on a tattooist's couch, ear-piercing is a ritual played out by teenagers seated in the windows of fashion jewellers such as *Claire's Accessories* the country over. Art jewellery, however, features something that pushes and pulls at this line, stretching and challenging our definitions of adornment, beauty and wearability. It provides a moment to measure up the visual cues we send out to others against the felt experience of our own embodied worlds, and to engage in dialogue those who catch our eye.

Sian Hindle

Maren Düsel
Hangloose Earrings
Sterling silver

© Christin Snyders

DELICATE

Marta Alonso
Dip oro tallo
Silver, gold plating, patina

◎ Mario Wurzburger

Marta Alonso
Dip oro círculo
Silver, gold plating, patina

◎ Mario Wurzburger

Míriam Alsina Climent
Pendientes Trapecio
Silver 925, gold 18 K, white
diamonds, black diamonds

◎ Arantxa Díez

Joana Santos
Raiz
Silver

Rossana Mendes Fonseca

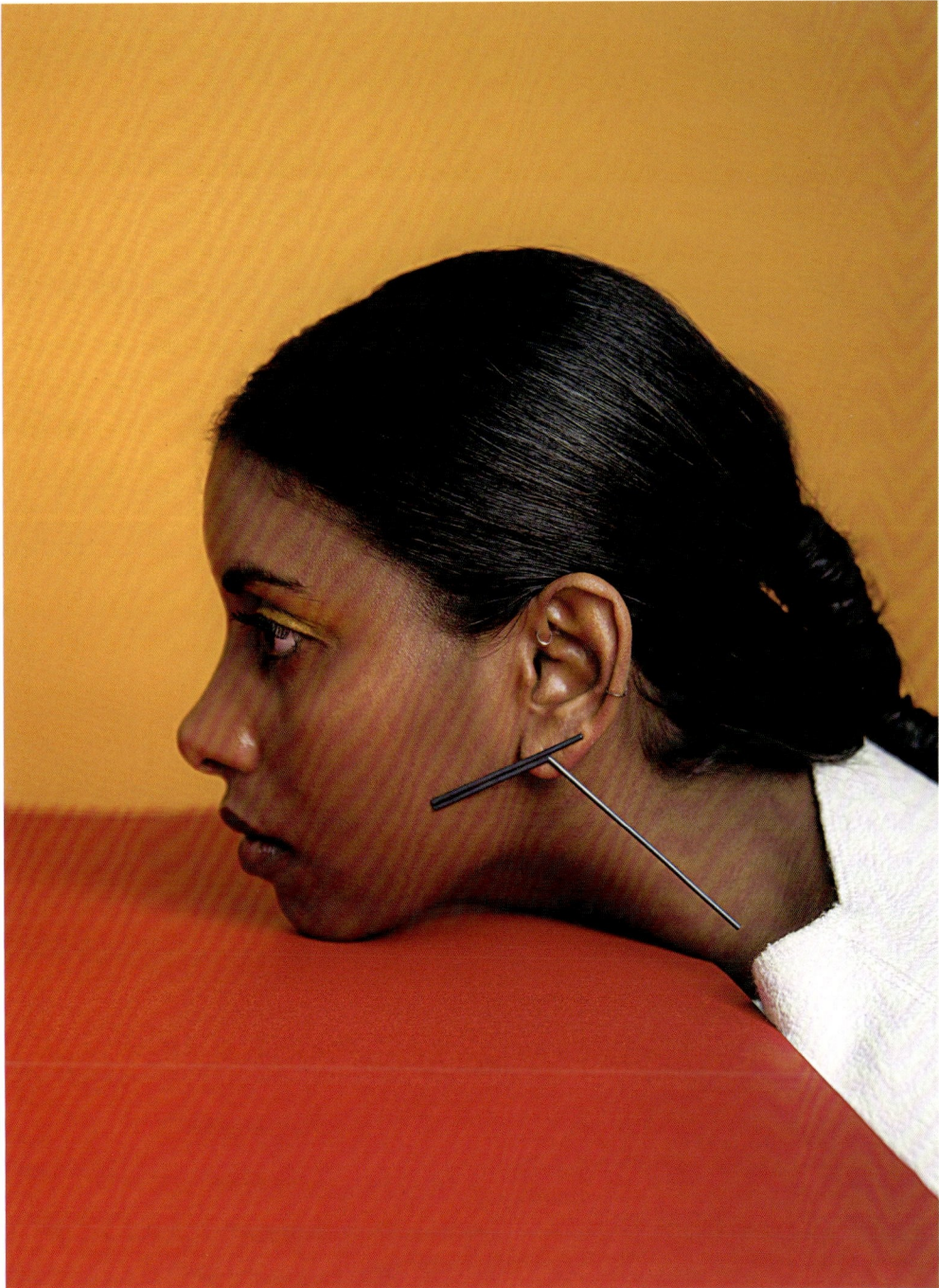

Joana Santos
Raiz
Silver

Rossana Mendes Fonseca

Berta Sumpsi
Clip
Silver
....
◎ Luis Villalba

Berta Sumpsi
Continuous
Silver
....
◎ Luis Villalba

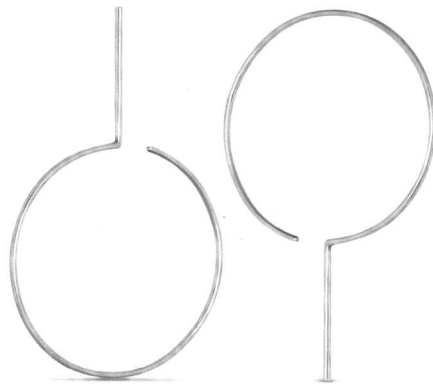

Berta Sumpsi
Question mark
Silver
....
◎ Luis Villalba

Ana Pina
Leku n. 5
Sterling silver

◎ By the artist

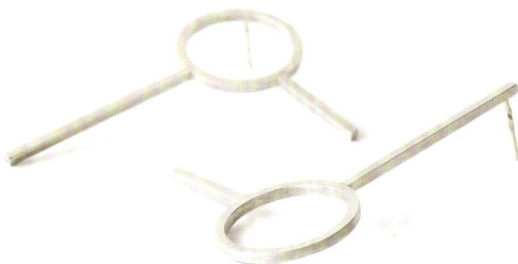

Ana Pina
Leku n. 4
Sterling silver

◎ By the artist

Dalila Gomes
Angled
Sterling silver

By the artist

Dalila Gomes
Parallel
Sterling silver

By the artist

Kira Huth
No.6
Sterling silver

By the artist

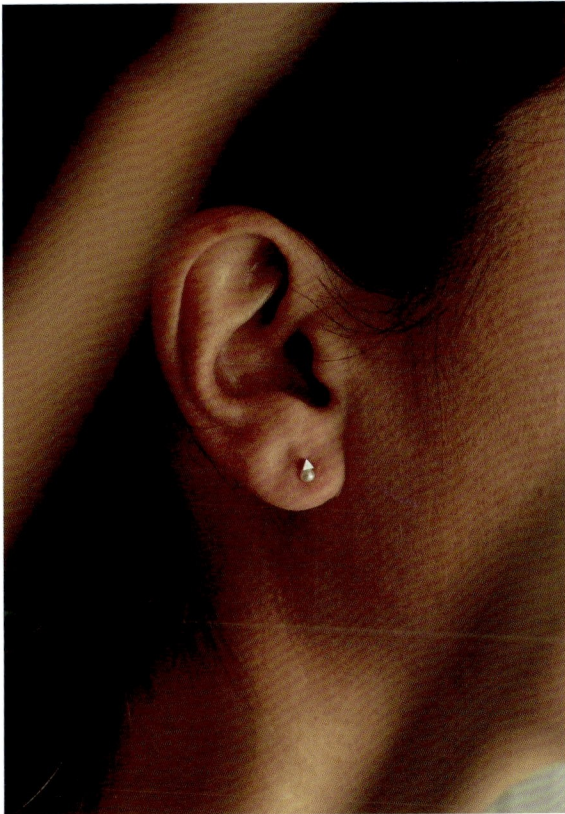

Sandra Llusà
Jara Seed Gold
Gold, pearl
....
⊙ Guillermo Portillo

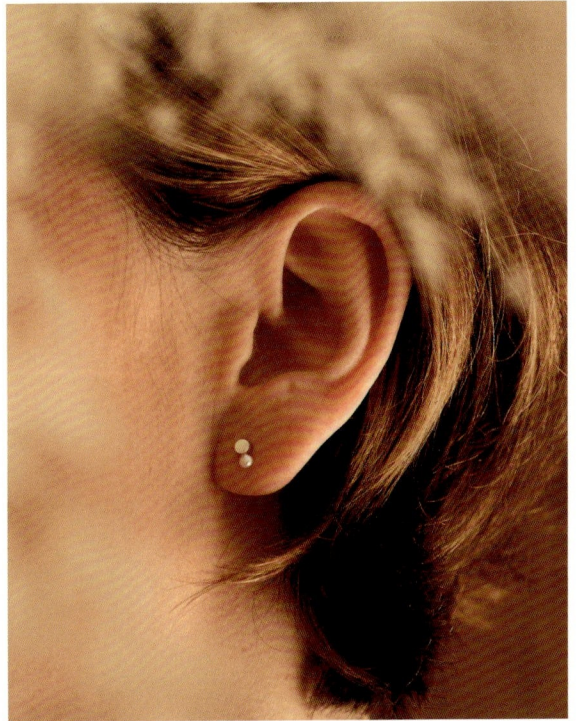

Sandra Llusà
Edelweiss seed
Silver, pearl
....
⊙ Guillermo Portillo

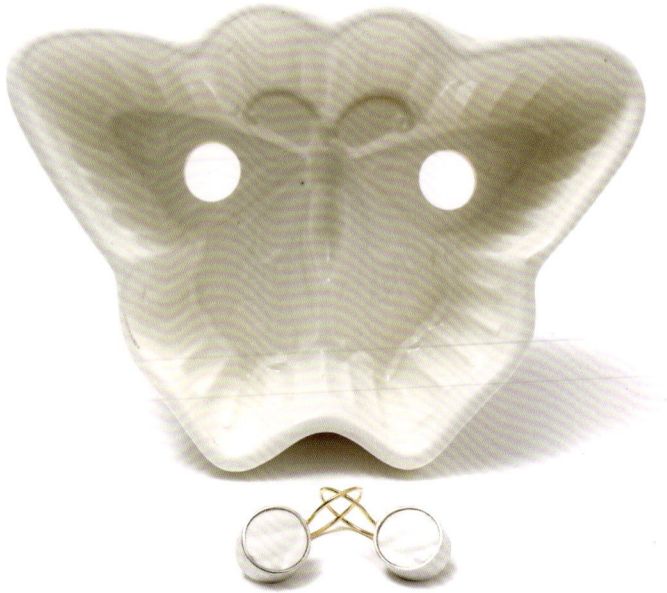

Gésine Hackenberg
Small Butterfly Earrings
Earthenware, 18 ct gold, silver

◎ By the artist

Catalina Rivera
Pendientes Otto
925 silver, gold plating, PLA
filament and elastic fabric

◎ María Planillo. Pixel Estudio

Vivian S.Q. Shi
Grenade
Silver, gold plated, pearl

◎ By the artist

Elvira Cibotti
Water
Recycled paper, silver
....
◎ Damian Wasser

Elvira Cibotti
Fire
Recycled paper, silver
....
◎ Damian Wasser

Laura Herrlich
Insectum
925/- silver & laquer
....
◎ Juliane Brandes

Ariadne Kapelioti
"Phaos" Ear Jackets
3D printed alumide,
colour dye, steel, silver 925,
goldplated brass
....
◎ By the artist

Jenny Llewellyn
Cluster Hoops –
Teal fade silicone
Silicone, pigment, silver

◎ By the artist

Jenny Llewellyn
Rainbow Earrings
Silicone, pigment, oxidised silver

◎ By the artist

Andrea Auer
Cherries
Bakelite, silver
....
◎ Daniela Beranek

Andrea Auer
Black cherries and torso
Bakelite, silver
....
◎ Daniela Beranek

Gabriela Sierra Torres
Globos
Silver, glass, quartz, paint
....
◎ By the artist

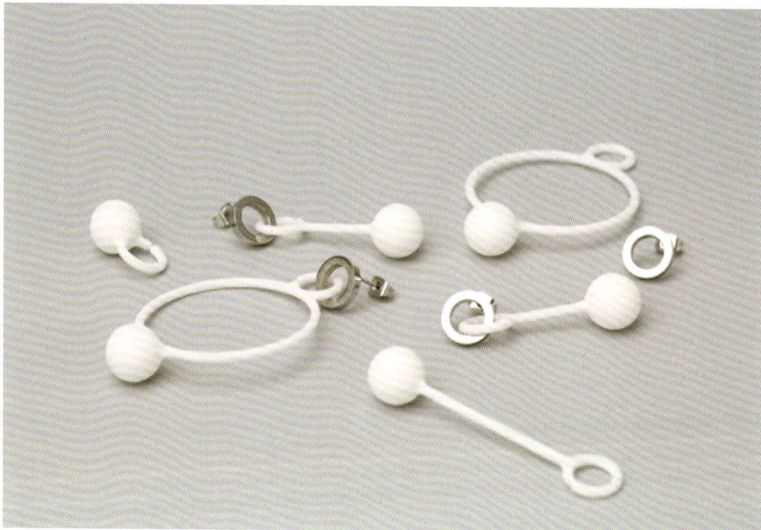

Dorothée Loustalot
Bubbles (magenta, white)
3D printed polyamid, sterling
silver
....
ⓘ Nicolas Lieber

Nóra Tengely
Too much Earrings
Patinated copper, freshwater
pearls, silver 925
....
◎ Marcell Piti

Nóra Tengely
Strong series
Patinated copper, freshwater
pearls, silver 925 silver
....
◎ Marcell Piti

Liisa Hashimoto
Green Awa Earring
Silver, acrylic paint
....
◎ Atsushi Hashimoto

Munay Martínez
Pendientes Racimo
Silver 925, freshwater pearls

⌾ Marcelo Pérez López

Nicolas Estrada
Florecitas
Silver, rock crystal, rose quartz,
blue topaz, pearls
....
⊙ Joan Soto

Nicolas Estrada
Rositas
Gold, rock crystal
....
⊙ Joan Soto

Violeta Adomaitytė
12 flowers
Gold, mother of pearl, silver
....
⊙ PhotoLab. lt

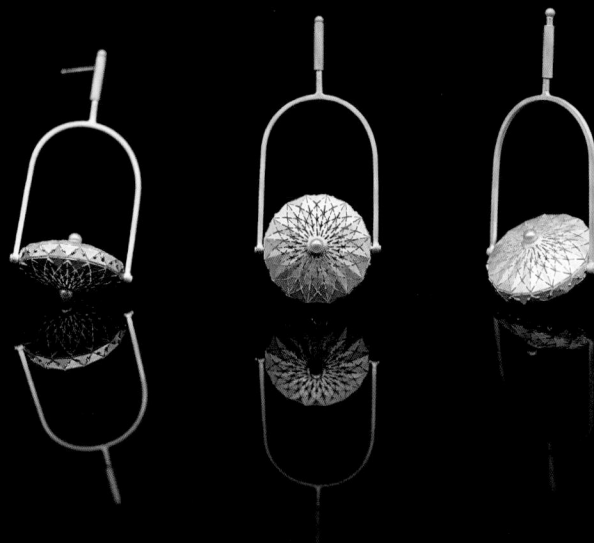

Xinia Guan
Infinity Earrings
Sterling silver, FW pearls
....
⊙ By the artist

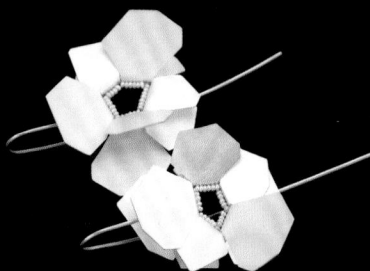

Isabelle Hertzeisen
Folded
Sterling silver, freshwater (junt)
....
⊙ By the artist

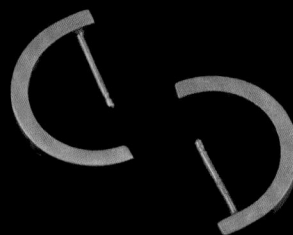

Ester Ferret
Arcus
Matte silver
....
⊙ Click by Ribelle Design
(P. Nagliero)

Kim Allwright
Planetary Dance
Earrings with Red Dwarf
Stoppers
Sterling silver, resin, silicon

◎ Paul Mounsey Photography

Kim Allwright
Rings of Saturn Studs
Sterling silver, resin

◎ Paul Mounsey Photography

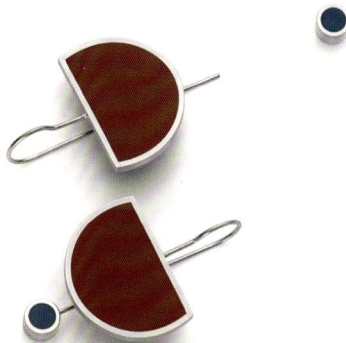

Kim Allwright
Eclipse Earrings with
Blue Moon Stoppers
Sterling silver, resin, silicone

◎ Paul Mounsey Photography

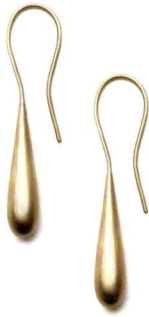

Olivia Shih
Liquid Gold Long Drop
Earrings
Recycled 14k gold

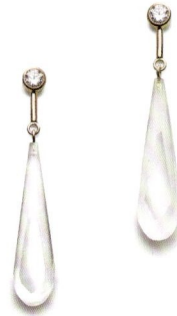

By the artist

Olivia Shih
Lucid Long Drop
Earrings
Recycled 14k gold, traceable
diamonds, hand carved rock
crystal

By the artist

Olivia Shih
Lucid Rock Earrings
Recycled 14k gold, traceable
diamonds, hand carved rock
crystal

By the artist

Olivia Shih
Lumen Curve Earrings
Recycled 14k gold, hand
carved rock crystal

By the artist

Olivia Shih
Lucid Asymmetrical
Line Studs
Recycled 14k gold, traceable
diamonds, hand carved rock
crystal

By the artist

Maria Avillez
Olive Branch Earrings
Silver goldplated
....
◎ Gonçalo Catarino

Maria Avillez
Peacock Feather
with Stone
Silver goldplated
....
◎ Gonçalo Catarino

Maria Avillez
Tears of Joy
Silver goldplated
....
◎ Gonçalo Catarino

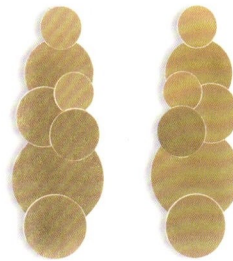

Maria Avillez
Bubbles Earrings
Silver goldplated
....
◎ Gonçalo Catarino

Yuki Sumiya
Structure
24K gold plating sterling
silver, rhodium plating sterling
silver, black rhodium plating
sterling silver

© Yuko Okoso

Uli Biskup Schmuck
Achter

Silver, gold, steel, coral, pearls, smoky quartz, gem beads

© Mirei Takeuchi

Uli Biskup Schmuck
Bubbles
Silver, steel, gem beads
⋯⋯⋯⋯⋯⋯⋯⋯⋯⋯⋯⋯
◎ Mirei Takeuchi

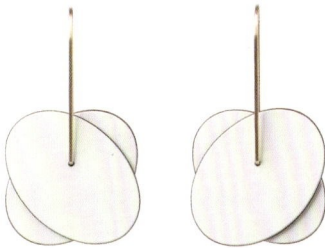

Uli Biskup Schmuck
In balance - white
Gold, HPL (high pressure
laminate)
⋯⋯⋯⋯⋯⋯⋯⋯⋯⋯⋯⋯
◎ Mirei Takeuchi

Uli Biskup Schmuck
In balance - red
Gold, HPL (high pressure
laminate)
⋯⋯⋯⋯⋯⋯⋯⋯⋯⋯⋯⋯
◎ Mirei Takeuchi

Els Vansteelandt
Cloud
Gold 18ct

◎ Bram Tack

Els Vansteelandt
Golden Line
Gold 18ct

◎ Bram Tack

Els Vansteelandt
Berry I
Silver 925, carnelian

◎ Bram Tack

Ana Cardim
Straight Ways
(Straight Collection)
Brass with satin treatment and
high-gloss polish, gold plated
finish

© Lena Wan

Ana Cardim
Long Leafs
(Ginkgo Collection)
Silver, high-gloss polishing
....
⊙ Lena Wan

Yeena Yoon
Covet Interactive
Pearl Drop
Sterling silver, gold, akoya pearl

◎ Richard Valencia

Yeena Yoon
Covet Pearl Earrings
Sterling silver, gold, akoya pearl

◎ Richard Valencia

Yeena Yoon
Covet Pearl Swing
Earrings
Sterling silver, gold, akoya pearl

◎ Richard Valencia

Donna D'Aquino
X-Large Circle
Structure Earrings
Steel / 18ky
....
◎ Ralph Gabriner

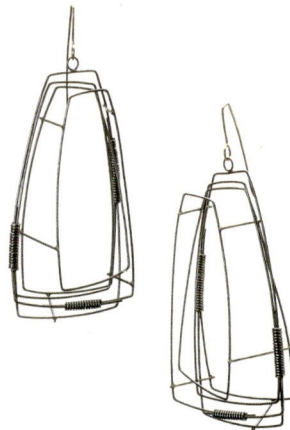

Donna D'Aquino
Rectangle Structure
Earrings
Steel / 18ky
....
◎ Ralph Gabriner

Donna D'Aquino
Chandelier Earrings
Steel / 18ky
....
◎ Ralph Gabriner

Michal Oren
Waterfall and Alice
Playing by the Pool
Oxidised silver, pearl

Roni Cnaani

Mar Sánchez
The Dark Side
Oxidised silver

Eric Parey

Vika Mayzel
Ocean Earrings
14K white gold

Alina Chopenko

Xinia Guan
Balloon Earrings
Argentium silver, sterling silver,
peridots

By the artist

Xinia Guan
Flatland Earring
24k gold plated sterling silver,
oxidised sterling silver

◎ Pistachios Gallery

Anna Vlahos
Ash Queen Earrings
Sterling silver

◎ By the artist

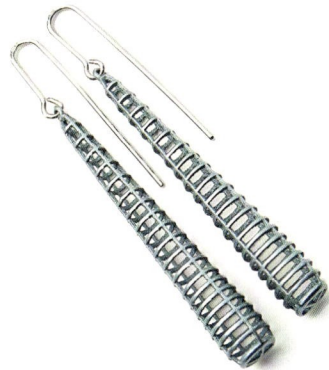

Stefania Lucchetta
Crystal
Anodised titanium and
white gold

◎ Fabio Zonta

Stefania Lucchetta
Cages
Anodised titanium and
white gold

◎ By the artist

Constanza Nolé
Alas
Enamelled bronze

© Dolores Esteve García

Constanza Nolé
Colmena
Enamelled bronze

© Dolores Esteve García

Anne Bader
Eldar
Sterling silver
....
◎ Stefano Zanini

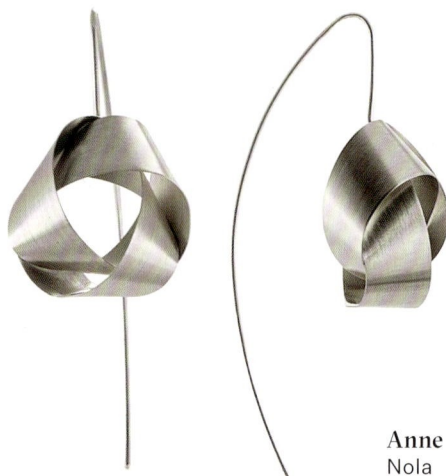

Anne Bader
Nola
Sterling silver
....
◎ Stefano Zanini

Kinga Sulej
Black n. 8
Silver

Bartek Zaranek

Kinga Sulej
Black n. 7
Silver

Bartek Zaranek

Ralph Bakker
YinYang
Silver tantalum

○ Michael Anhalt

Ralph Bakker
Pearl Grapes
Gold pearls

○ Michael Anhalt

Ralph Bakker
Bamboo
Gold silver enamel

○ Michael Anhalt

Ralph Bakker
LaStanze1
Gold lens

○ Michael Anhalt

Roc Majoral
Party
8kt Fairmined gold

◎ Majoral

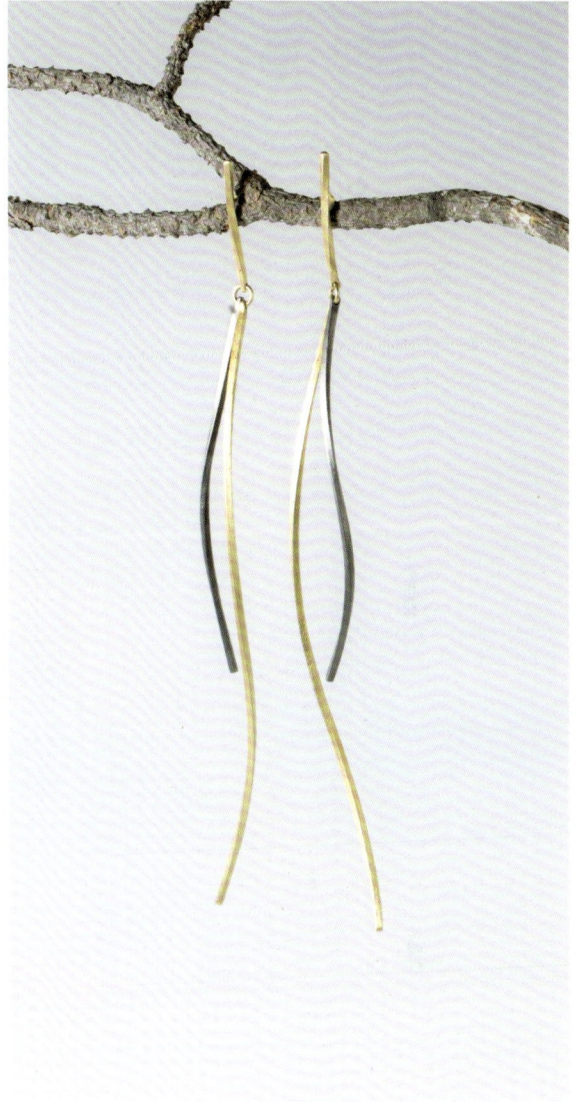

Roc Majoral
Pinassa
18kt Fairmined gold and Titanium

◎ Majoral

Tass Joies
Annabel Lee
Sterling silver with matte
gold-plated finish

◎ Anna Poch

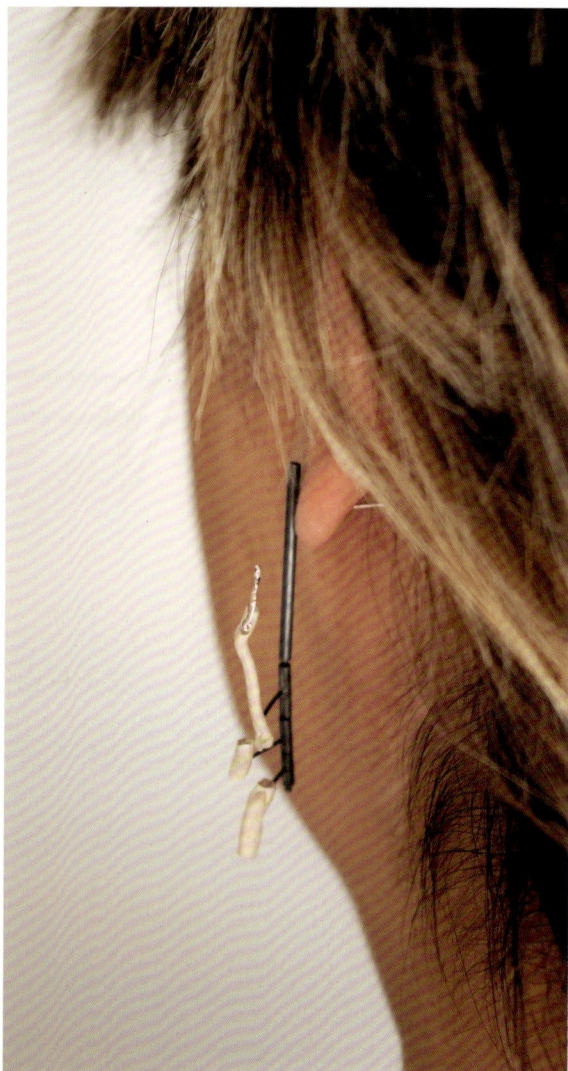

Anna Rafecas
Herramientas para
el alma. Brote n. 1
Sterling silver, boxwood
and hot enamel

◎ Duna Romagosa

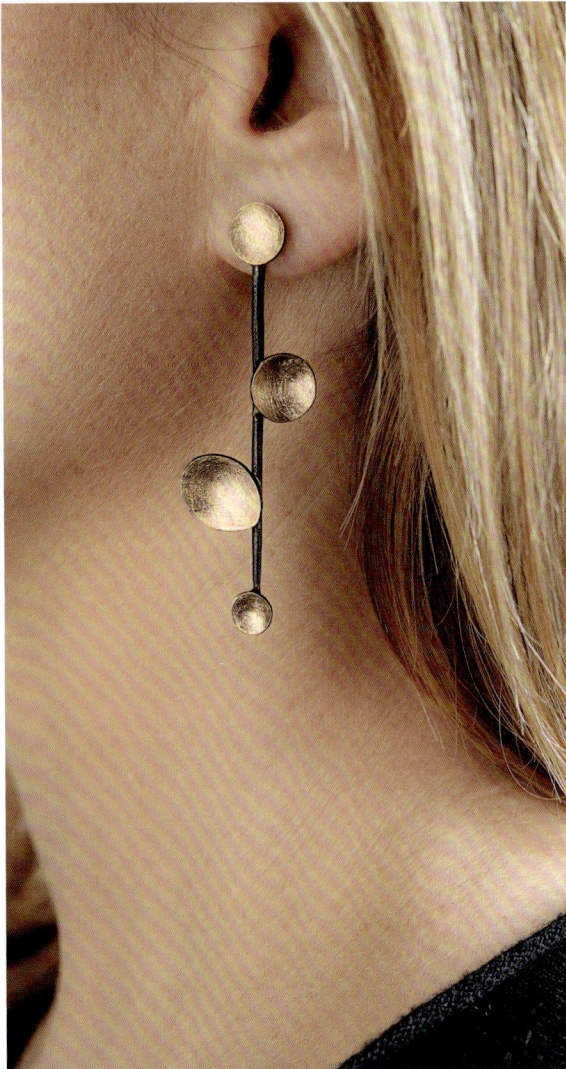

Corrado De Meo
Concave
Oxided silver, 14kt gold
....
Federico Cavicchioli

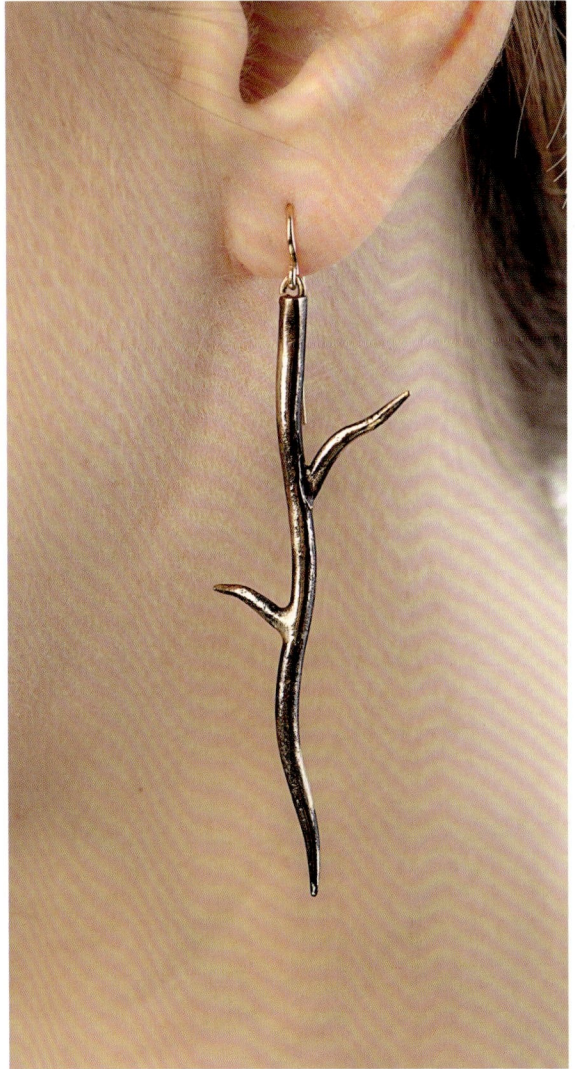

Corrado De Meo
Spine
Bronze, 18kt gold
....
Federico Cavicchioli

Selma Leal
Lady Musgrave
Collection
Silver, enamel
....
◉ Gemma Pinedo

Inesa Kovalova
Morphology
Nylon, gold vermeil, gold leaf
....
◉ By the artist

Oles Tsura
Untitled
Mushroom, stainless steel
....
◉ By the artist

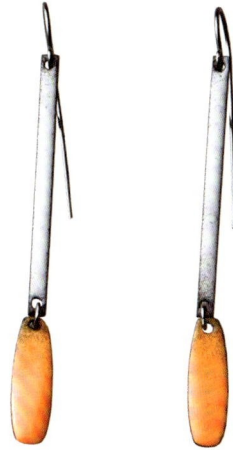

Julia Turner
Camilla Earrings
Steel, vitreous enamel, silver

◎ By the artist

Terhi Tolvanen
Grass
Reconstructed jade,
tourmaline, silver

◎ By the artist

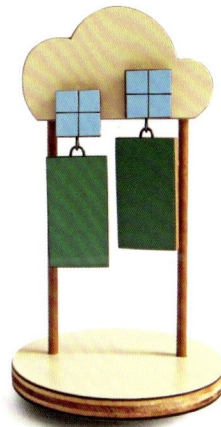

Karen Vanmol
Stilleven, In the middle
of the street
Wood, laminate, silver

◎ By the artist

Beate Pfefferkorn
Field of Flowers
Porcelain, sterling silver,
wood
....
By the artist

Liaung Chung
Blossom earrings #2
18 yellow gold, diamonds
....
Shu Ching Yang

Liaung Chung
Blossom earrings #3
18 yellow gold, rhodocrosite,
pearls
....
Shu Ching Yang

Erica Bello
Long Stemmed Flowers
Oxidised silver, 18k gold,
bloodstone
....
◉ By the artist

Erica Bello
Potted Plants
Oxidised silver
....
◉ By the artist

Anna Vlahos
Kachnar Earrings
Sterling silver
....
◉ By the artist

Chao-Hsien Kuo
Sparkling Forest
Silver, gold, pearls
....
◉ By the artist

Lucy Spink
Lichen Statement
Silver, gold
....
◎ Darren Newbury

Chao-Hsien Kuo
Sunbeams
Gold, pearls
....
◎ By the artist

Esperança Leria
Terra Viva (Alive Earth)
earrings
Pearl, 950 silver cast palm branches
worked by hands
....
⊙ Liliane Melo

Marina Sheetikoff
Arruda Earring
Niobium anodized

⊙ By the artist

Caroline Lindholm
Gold Floral Ornament
Gold, pearls
....
⊙ Niklas Palmklint

Caroline Lindholm
Round Floral Ornament
Oxidised silver with blue
freshwaterpearls
....
⊙ Niklas Palmklint

Martina Obid Mlakar
Feeling free
Silver 925/000

Tadej Čaušević

Gabriele Hinze
Wings
Fine silver, sterling silver

◎ Simon Wolf

Martina Obid Mlakar
Ginkgo
Titanium

◎ Anton Mlakar

Edna Madera
N. 259 Feather
Gold, silver

◎ Cole Rodger

Andrea Vaggione
Panambi
Stainless steel, silver

◎ Vincent_ramet

Edwin Charmain
Pattra Earstuds
Fine silver, recycled silver
(sterling)

By the artist

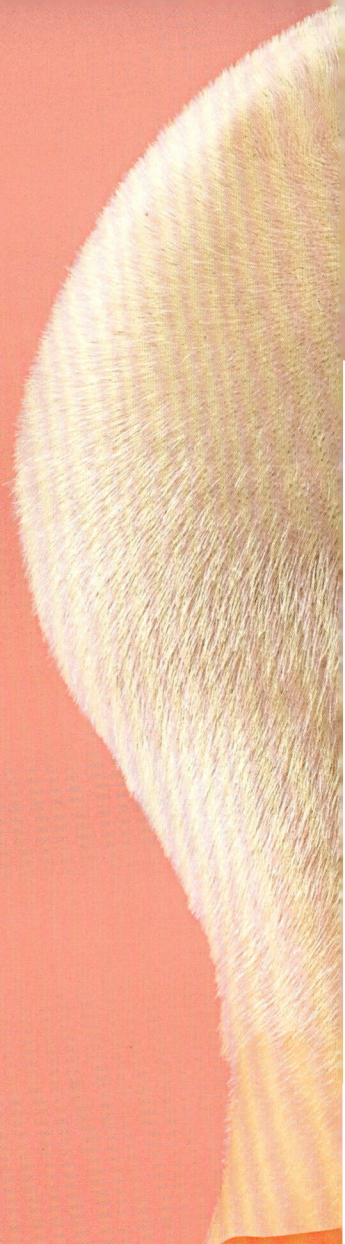

SOLID

Jo Pudelko
Cloud Periphery Earrings
Powder coated steel, acrylic
with Sterling silver findings

© Stacey Bentley

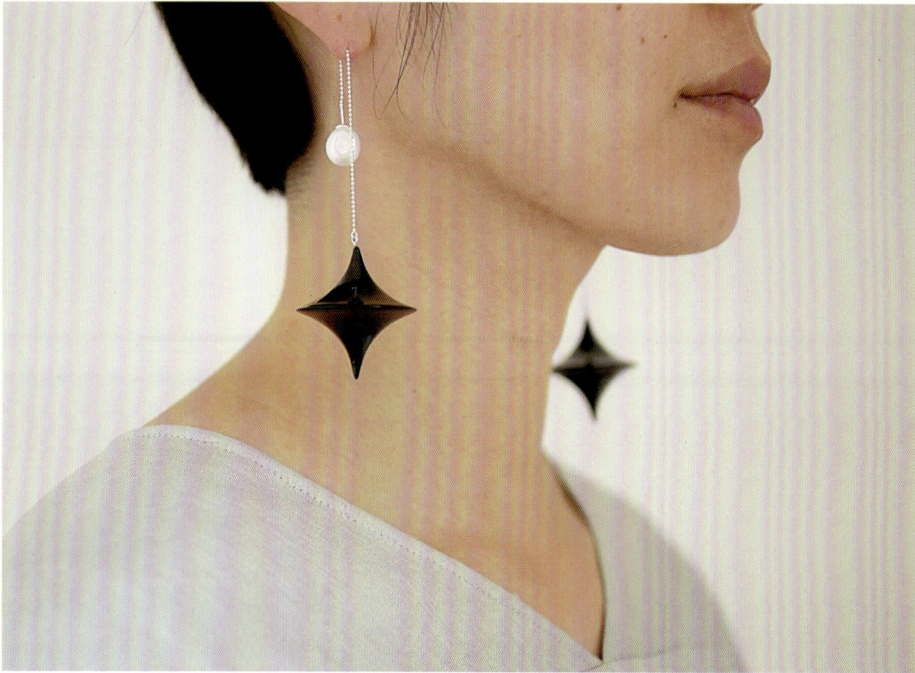

Misato Seki
Planet
Urushi, Japanese paper,
silver, resin, pearl

Daisuke Kato

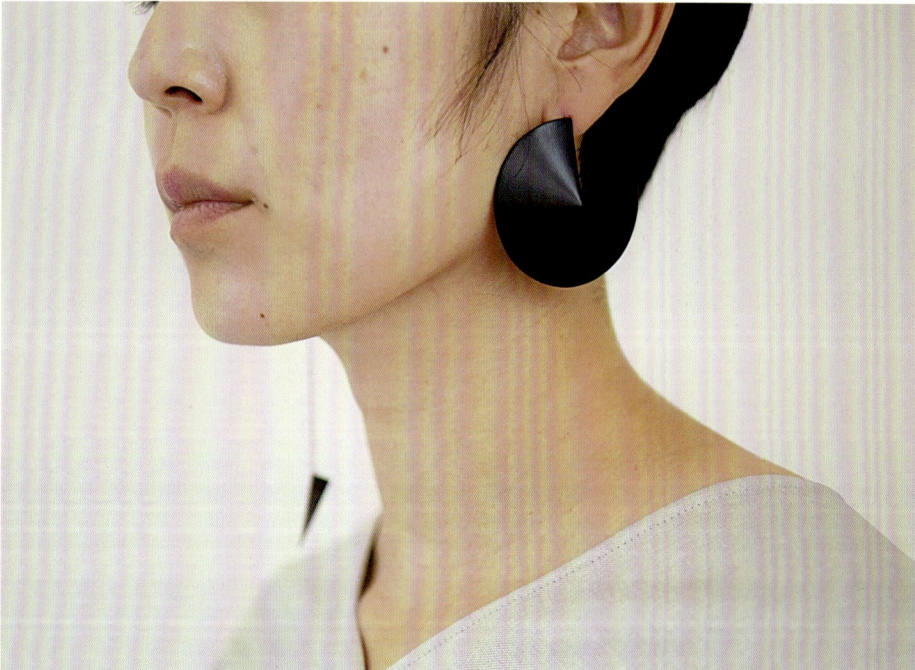

Misato Seki
Fragment
Urushi, hemp cloth,
Japanese paper, silver

Daisuke Kato

Tass Joies
Pètals
Oxidized sterling silver
with natural diamonds

⊙ Mireia Rodriguez

Stephanie Jendis
Earjewels: Vlinders
Ebony, 18kt gold

⊙ Oliver Mann

Michelle Kraemer
Bold minimalism
Balsa wood, paint,
pigments, varnish

© Christoph Schubert

Silvia Bellia
Blowing a kiss
Cacholong, reconstructed
coral, silver

◎ By the artist

Silvia Bellia
Edgy
Basalt

◎ By the artist

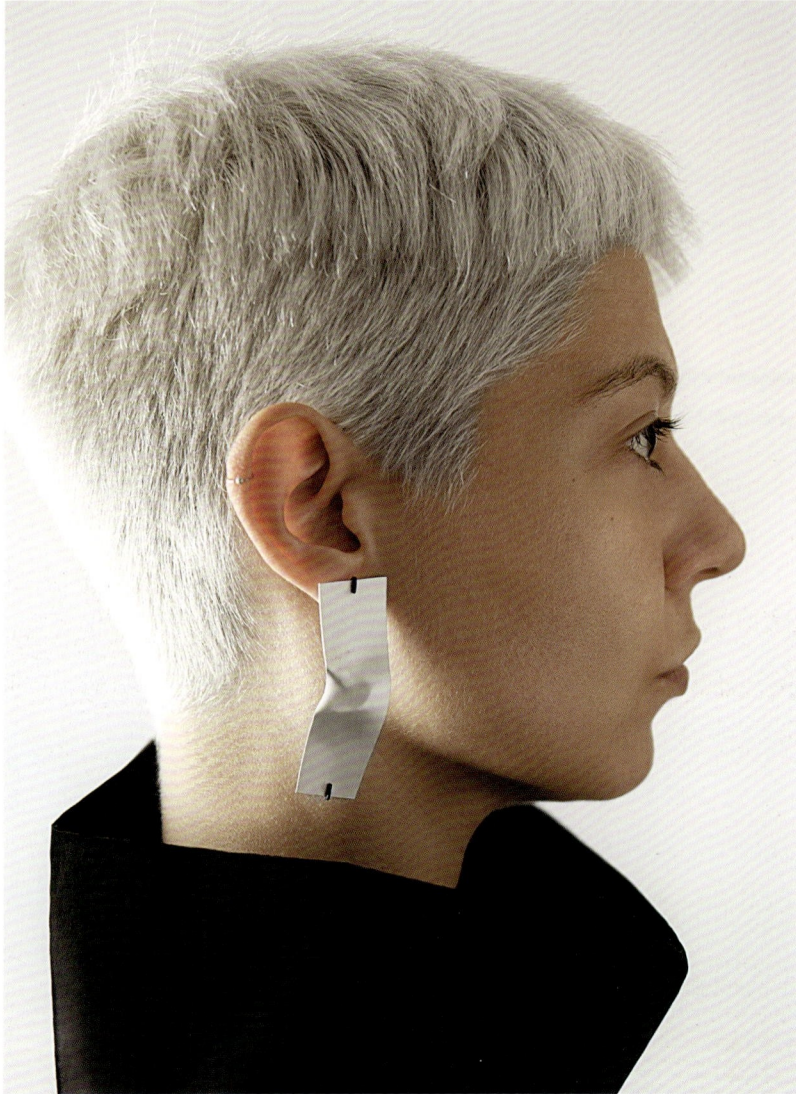

Joana Santos
Milk
Silver, polymer

◎ Rossana Mendes Fonseca

Esperança Leria
Cheio|Vazio (Full|Empty)
950 silver

Patricia Ikeda

Xiao Chen
B. O.
Fluorescent methyl
methacrylate, silver, patina,
gilt, nitrile
....
Pierre Hilpert

Christoph Straube
BlueCuboids
Stainless steel, enamel,
white gold
....
By the artist

Nicolas Estrada
Ágata
Silver, agate
....
Joan Soto

Christoph Straube
PinkCuboids
Stainless steel, enamel,
yellow gold
....
By the artist

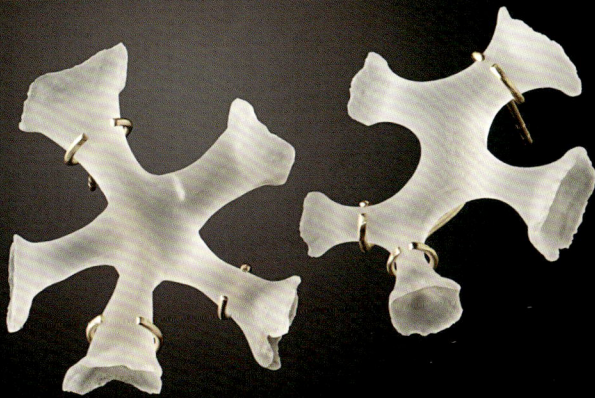

Nicolas Estrada
Spores n. 2 - Front and Back
Gold, rock crystal

....

◎ Joan Soto

Nicolas Estrada
Aqua
Gold, aquamarines

....

◎ Joan Soto

Nicolas Estrada
Trapiches
Gold, diamonds, trapiche emeralds

....

◎ Joan Soto

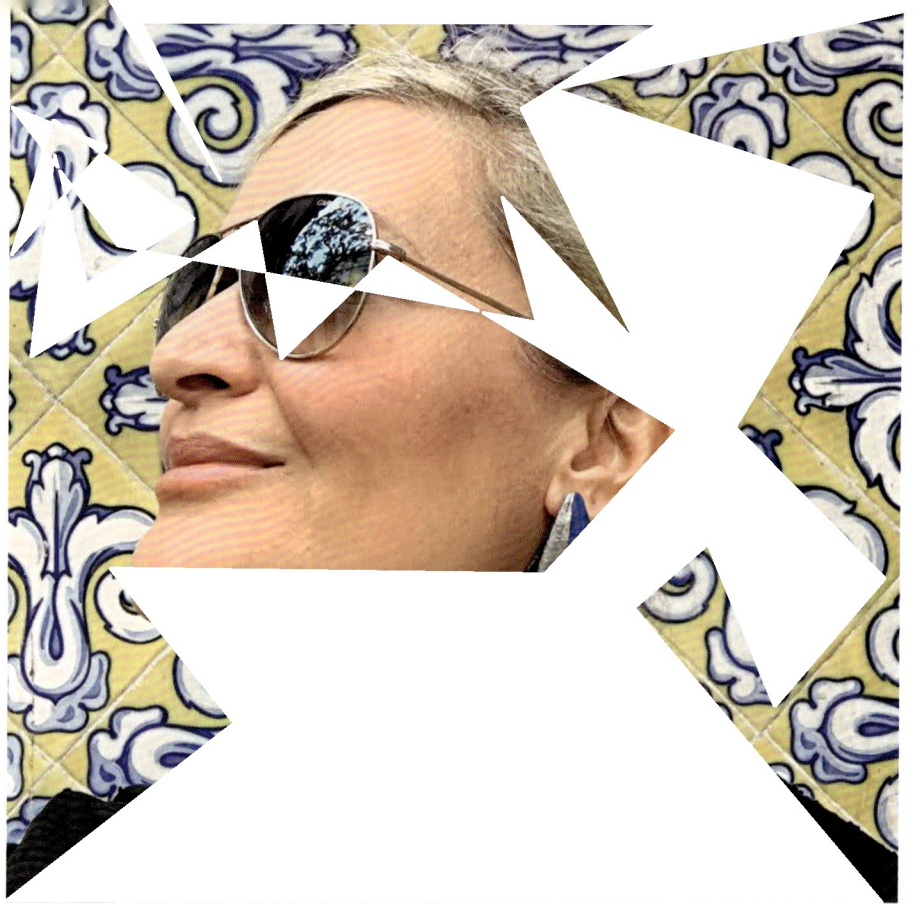

Burku Sülek
Feast
Papier mache, silver
....
◎ By the artist

Burku Sülek
Magnolias of Istanbul
Papier mache, silver
....
◎ Umut Töre

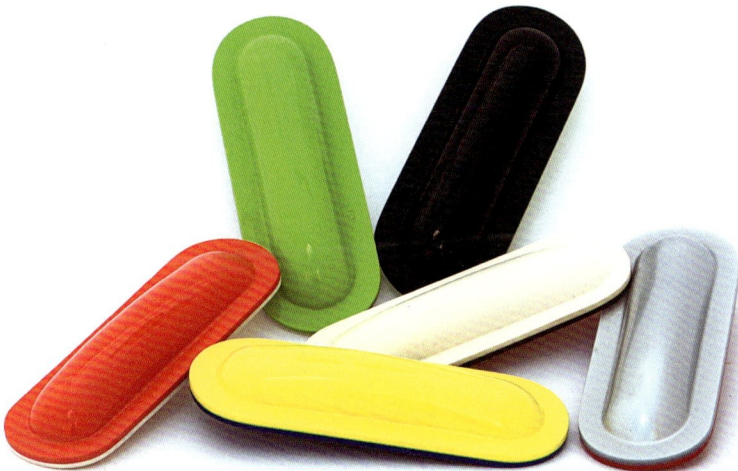

Ignasi Cavaller Triay
#FREEDON'T
Cellulose acetate and silver

By the artist

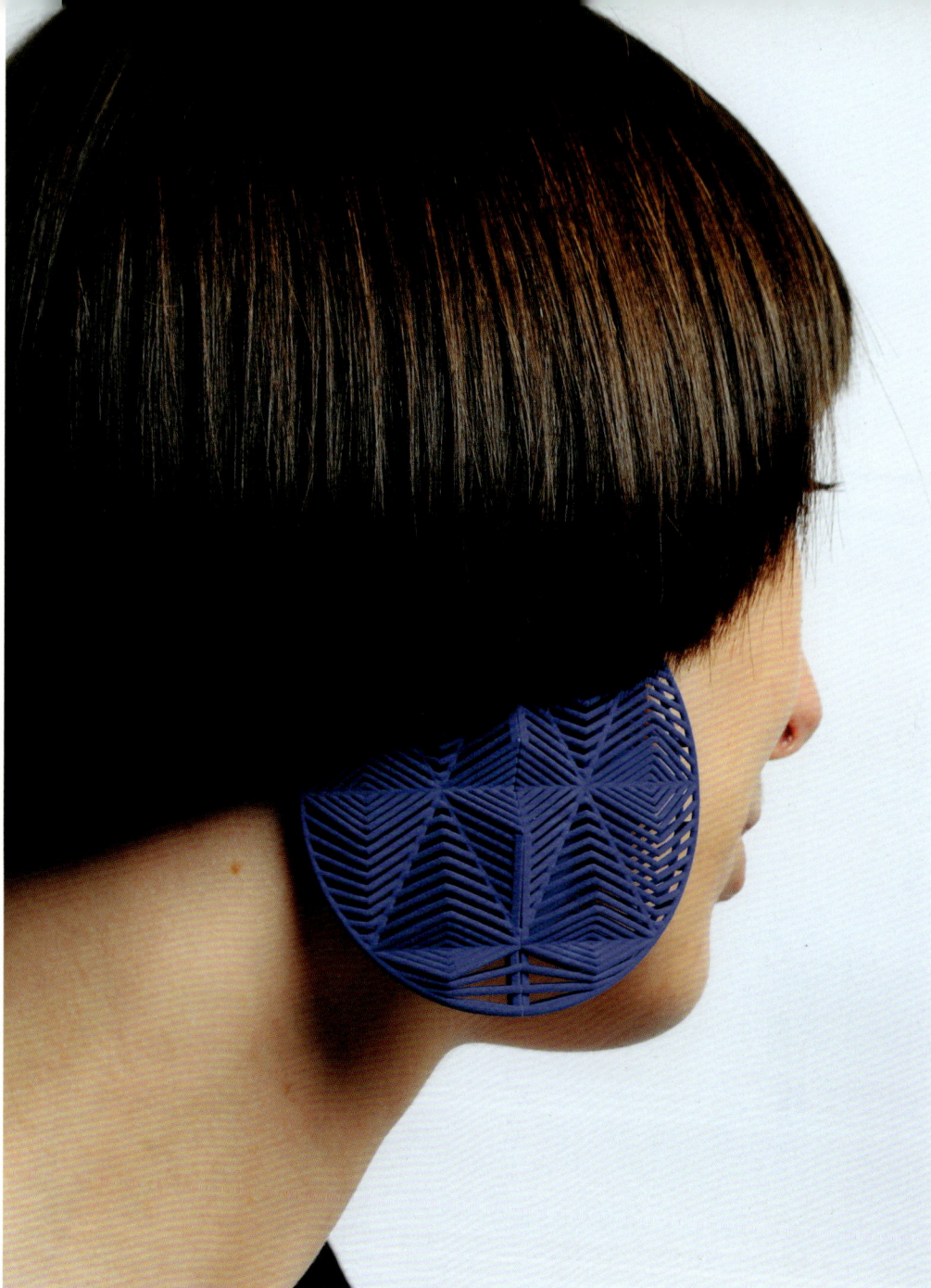

Theresa De Jager
Amashaza No.1
Hand dyed Nylon, sterling silver
and magnets

◎ By the artist

Valeria D'Annibale
Hoop Earrings XL
(pink)
Nylon, silver

© Nataliya Volosovych

Marina Sheetikoff
Luna
Anodised niobium

Pedro Fonseca

Giulia Savino
Istantanea Asian n. 2
Gold plated brass and silver,
powder coated brass
....
By the artist

Michelle Kraemer
Sunspots × saecula
Balsa wood, gold leaf,
goldplated silver

◎ Sofia Kabelka

Helena Aguilar
Arete disco
Powder-coated bronze
....
Andres Acosta

Eugènia Arnavat
Esferas
Silver and reconstituted turquoise
....
◎ Eric Parey

Liaung Chung
Rock earrings #2
18 yellow gold, 925 silver
....
◎ Shu Ching Yang

Elgin Fischer
Glade duo
Silver, vitreous enamel
....
◎ Zeitform Medien

Elgin Fischer
Glade
Silver, vitreous enamel
....
◎ Zeitform Medien

Sofia Beilharz
Big Courbe
Silver

Ⓒ Melanie Warnstaedt

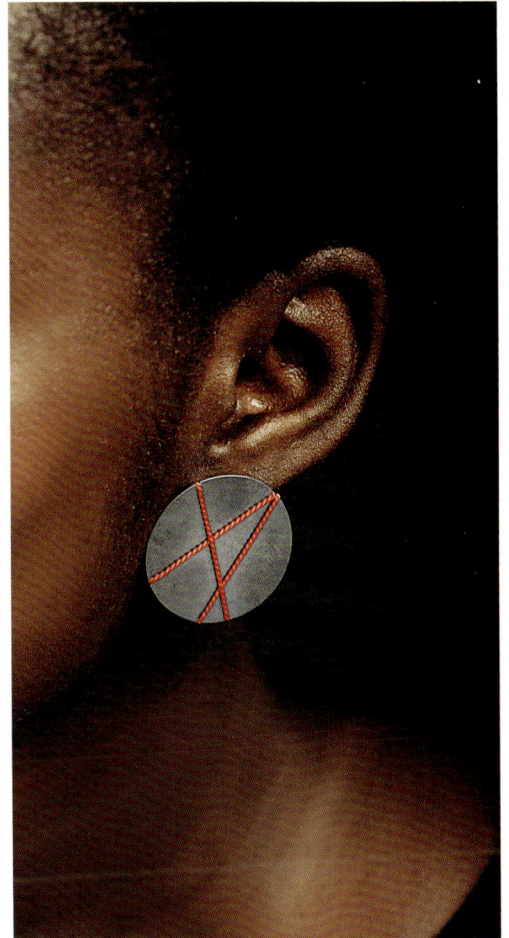

Sofia Beilharz
Big Disk black and red
Silver, blackened, silk cord

Ⓒ Melanie Warnstaedt

Marta Ortí
Flor
Porcelain and silver

◎ Cristina Orús

Denis Music
Fornax Earrings,
Black Hole collection
Black vintage silver, 14k gold

◎ By the artist

Denis Music
Idol Earrings,
Reinformation collection
Black vintage silver

◎ By the artist

Marta Ortí
Encreuaments
Porcelain and silver
....
○ Cristina Orús

Clara Niubò
NV-20
Brass, silver, gold

◎ Guillermo Portillo

Clara Niubò
SC-3
Silver, paint

◎ Guillermo Portillo

Sandra Enterline
Scalloped Oval Glass
Earring
Steel, oxidized sterling silver,
glass
....
◎ Mark Johann

Sandra Enterline
Mica Oval Drop Earring
Oxidised sterling silver, mica
....
◎ Mark Johann

Jenny Reeves
Opal Wing Earrings
Argentium sterling silver,
23K keum-boo, opal doublet,
white diamonds
....
◎ By the artist

Jennie Gill
Jet & Ruby
Whitby jet, oxidised silver,
ruby

◎ Jerry Lampson

Jennie Gill
Raw Whitby Jet
Whitby jet, oxidised silver,
yellow sapphire

◎ Jerry Lampson

Jennie Gill
Studs
Whitby jet, 18ct, diamond

◎ Jerry Lampson

Philip Sajet
B-52
Silver, covered with niello,
gold, 18crt

◎ Aatjan Renders

Dot Melanin
Mortar rain
Grenadil wood, silver,
quartz crystal, paint

◎ By the artist

Stephanie Jendis
Earjewels
Amethyst, buffalo horn,
oxidised silver

◎ Oliver Mann

Maria Rosa Franzin
Redviolet
Silver, coral, resin

⌖ By the artist

Cappy Counard
Mend
Silver, gold

⌖ By the artist

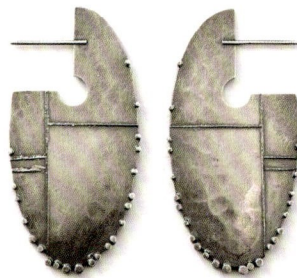

Cappy Counard
Patch
Sterling Silver

⌖ By the artist

Lavinia Rossetti
Alternating Ryhthm
Aluminum, silver

◎ Claudia Giglio

Chok Shin Ni
Aegis #4
Oxidised sterling silver, 9k gold

◎ By the artist

Valentina Falchi
Ninfa Earcuff
Gold-plated bronze

Raúl Mellado

Isabelle Hertzeisen
Ultima Forsan
18ct gold, beech wood
....
◉ Raphaël Rigoli

Isabelle Hertzeisen
Ultima Forsan
18ct gold, beech wood
....
◉ Raphaël Rigoli

Kamilė Stanelienė
Nostalgia II
Silver, tiles, freshwater pearls

⊙ Tautvydas Stanelis

Kamilė Stanelienė
New Stories II
Copper, plexiglass, silver, print

⊙ Tautvydas Stanelis

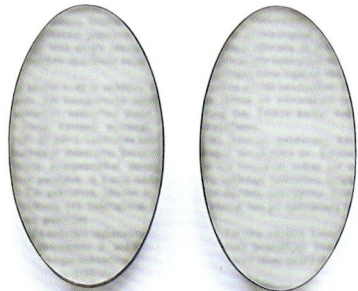

Kamilė Stanelienė
New Stories I
Copper, plexiglass, silver, print

⊙ Tautvydas Stanelis

Kim Shin_Ryeong
b.f.no15
925 silver, nickel silver

◉ Park Kwang-chan

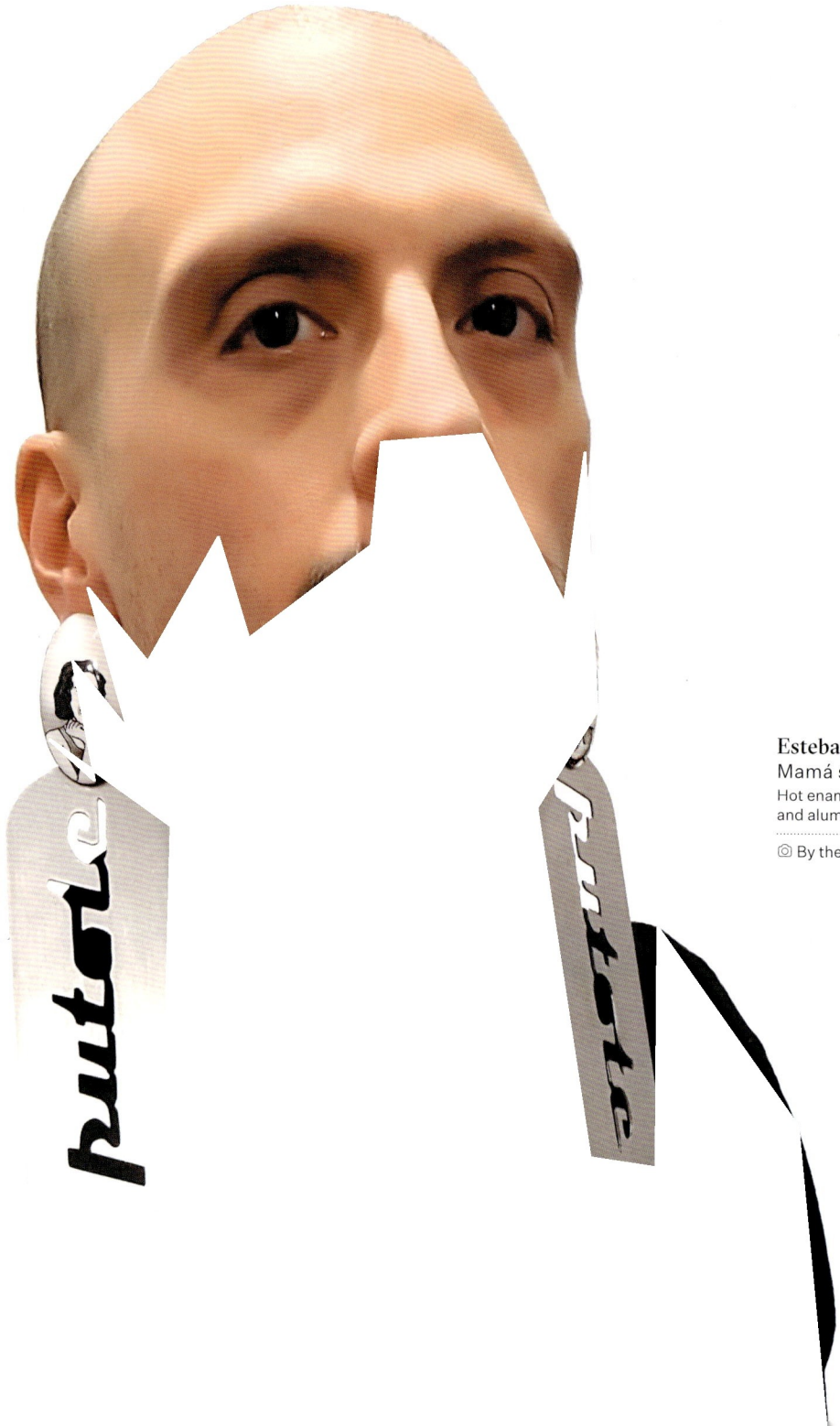

Esteban Erosky
Mamá soy gay!!
Hot enamel on copper
and aluminium

By the artist

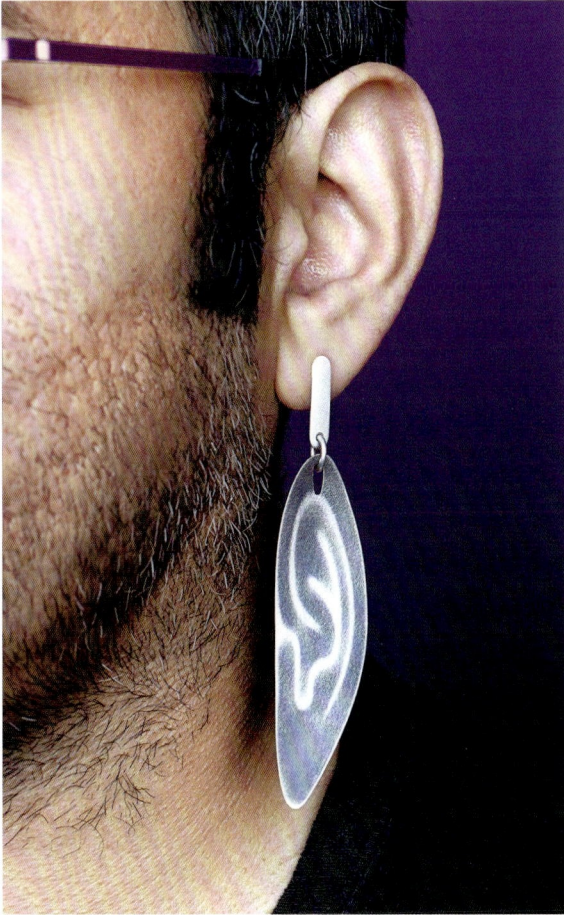

Stefan Gougherty
Stretched Ear Earrings
Sterling silver, stainless steel

....

By the artist

Stefan Gougherty
35 Cent Earrings
U.S. quarter stretched 400%,
U.S. dime, sterling silver

....

By the artist

Heidemarie Herb
Upcycled
Silver, gold, sapphire
....
By the artist

Nicole Schuster
Buds Blue
925 silver oxidised, titanium
....
By the artist

Nicole Schuster
Wallflower
925 silver oxidised, emeralds
....
By the artist

Karen Konzuk
Unity X Earrings (L)
Concrete and stainless steel

Cole Rodger Photographics

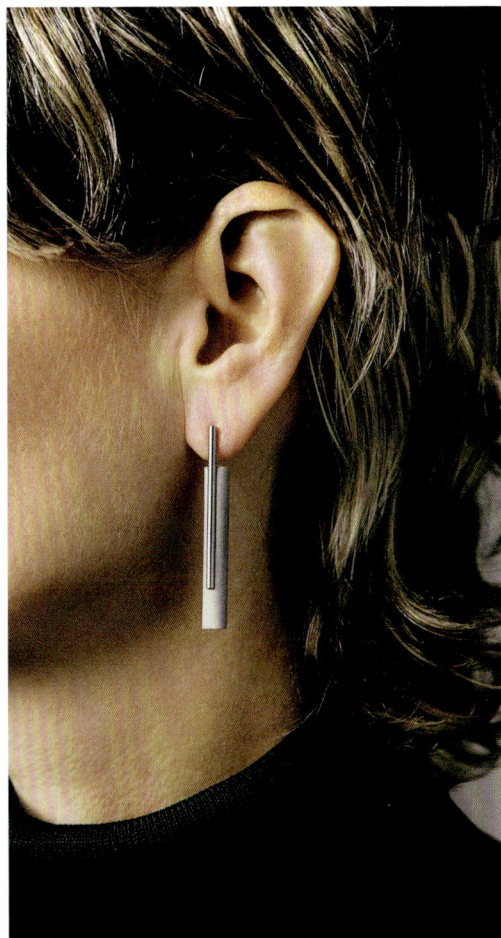

Karen Konzuk
Unity Tandem Earrings
Concrete and stainless steel

Cole Rodger Photographics

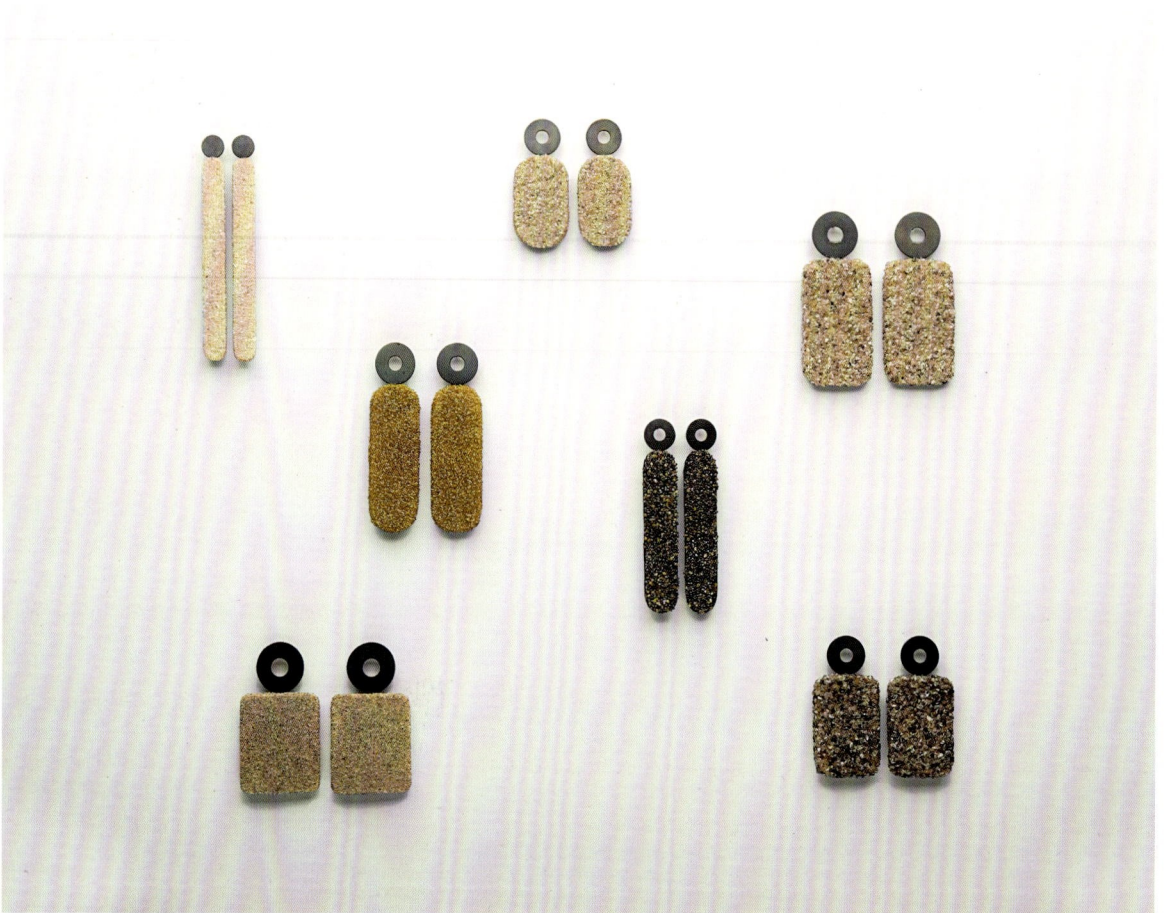

Ute Eitzenhöfer
Diamondpowderearrings
2014-a-g
Diamond powder, wood,
blackened silver
....
◎ Michael Müller

Heather Guidero
Carved Tab Link Earrings
Oxidised sterling silver
◎ Cole Rodger

Terhi Tolvanen
Pyrite Construction
Cherry wood, paint, silver,
reconstructed opal
◎ By the artist

Biba Schutz
1-FF-1
Patinated bronze
◎ Ron Boszko

Biba Schutz
1-FF-2
Patinated sterling silver
◎ Ron Boszko

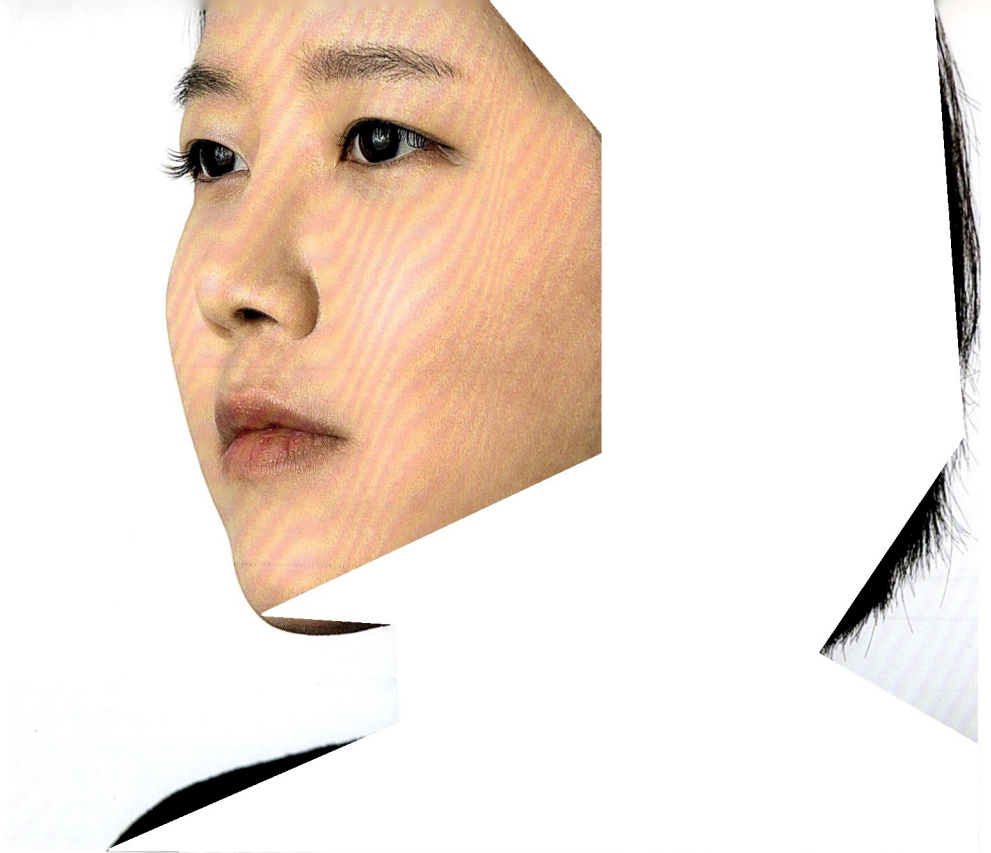

Jina Lee
Thick-ringed Earrings
24K gold, fine silver,
sterling silver

◎ Kwang-Choon Park

Teresa Milheiro
Testtube 1
Oxidised silver

◎ Luis Cunha Pais

Teresa Milheiro
Needle
Recycled needle

◎ Luis Cunha Pais

Anja Berg

Como las sábanas blancas

Green marble of Prato
and shibuichi

·····································

Marco Piunti

Carmen López
My mother's pearls 05
Enamel, cultured pearls, silver
....
⊙ Carmen Campos

EXPRESSIVE

Monica Krexa
Huracán
Aluminum, steel

© Doiss Messeder

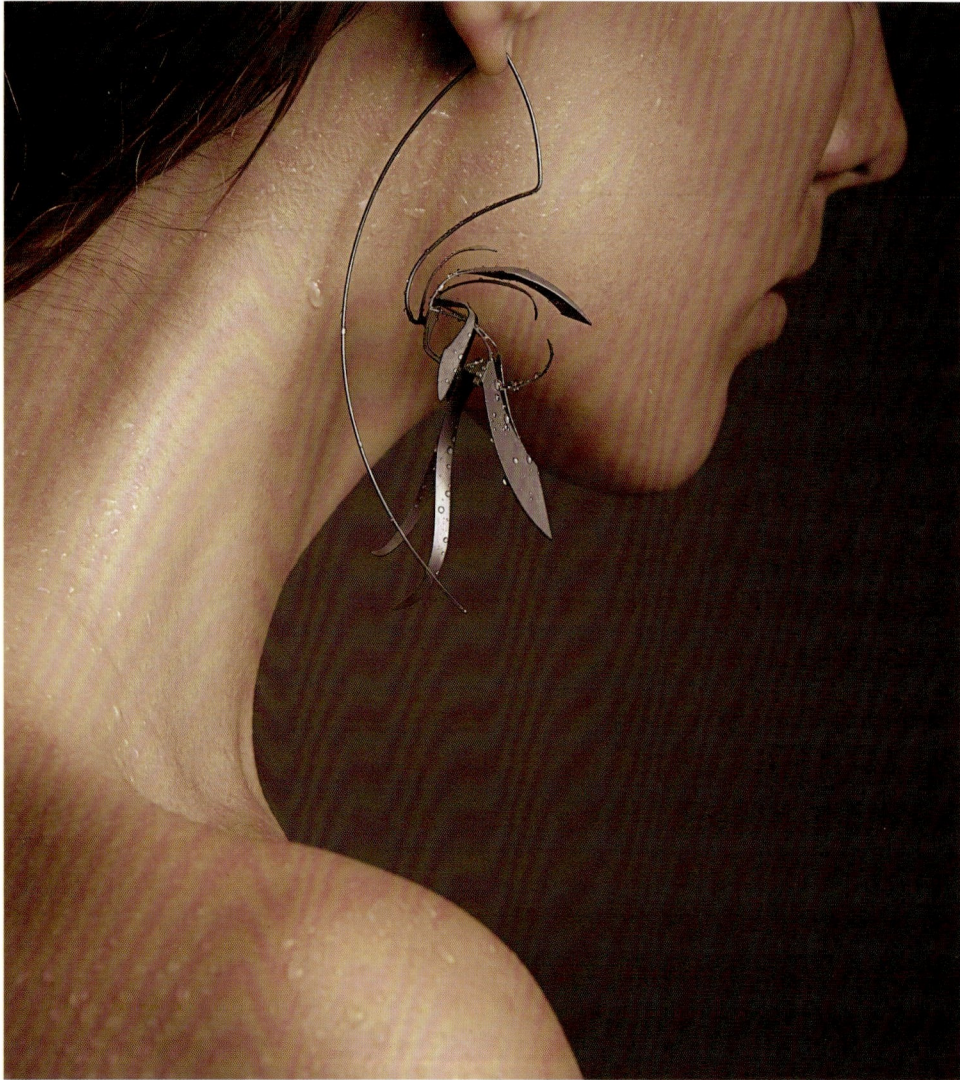

Kinga Sulej
Black n. 1
Silver

○ Bartek Zaranek

Ute Decker
Geometric Poetry
18kt fairtrade gold, stand

Jamie Trounce

Claudia Vallejo
1346, Abrir Espacio
collection
Scrap steel from industrial
processes with 22kt gold
plating

○ Camilo George

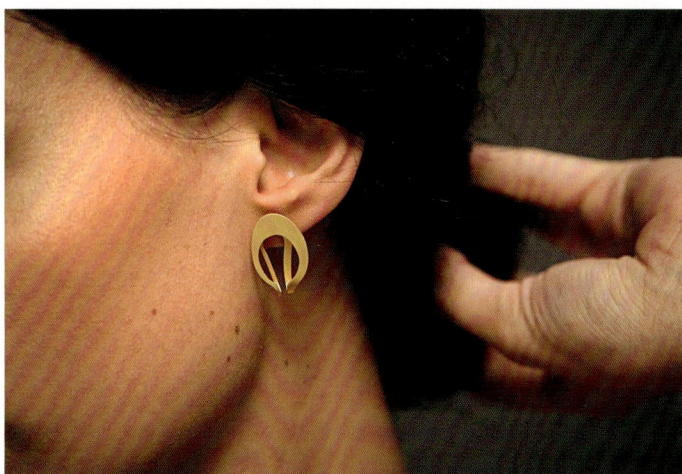

Claudia Vallejo
1348 Abrir Espacio
collection
Scrap steel from industrial
processes with 22kt gold
plating

○ Camilo George

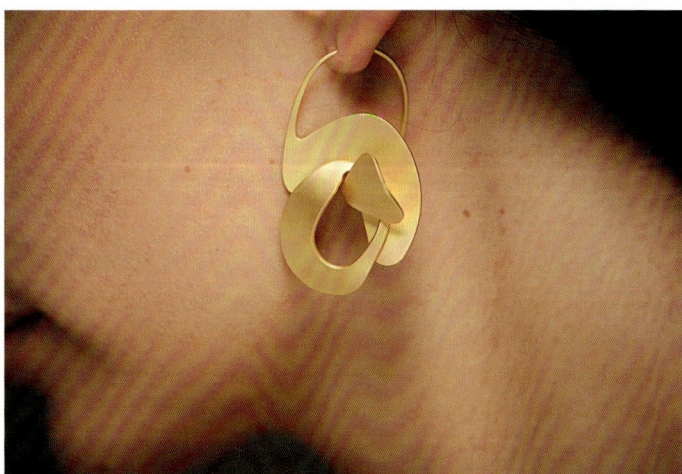

Claudia Vallejo
1298 Abrir Espacio
collection
Scrap steel from industrial
processes with 22kt gold
plating

○ Camilo George

Iris Saar
X2 Plunge Earrings
Stainless steel, 22ct matt gold
plate, black powder coat
....
⊙ By the artist

Iris Saar
X2 Puff Hoop Earrings
Stainless steel, 22ct matt gold
plate, black powder coat
....
⊙ By the artist

Iris Saar
X2 Aerial Earrings
Stainless steel, 22ct matt gold
plate, black powder coat
....
⊙ By the artist

Iris Saar
X2 Hang Stud Earrings
Stainless steel, 22ct matt gold
plate, black powder coat
....
⊙ By the artist

Eero Hintsanen
Stinger
Silver, gold foil

◎ Chao-Hsien Kuo

Eero Hintsanen
Flare
Silver

Lari Heikkilä

Olga Košica and Rok Mar
Flamboyant
Polyamide

◎ Mimi Antolović

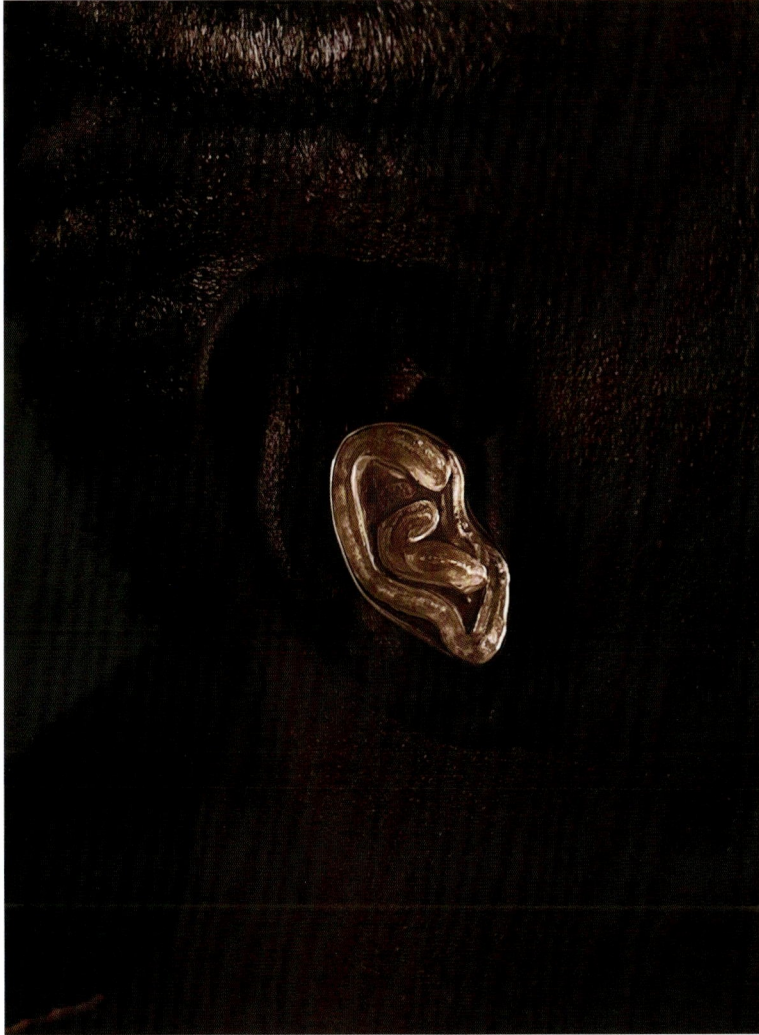

Sarah Al Manea
Voices
Silver

By the artist

Clara del Papa
Bejuca
925 silver, enamel, 24 kt gold
....
⊙ Daniele Dal Monte

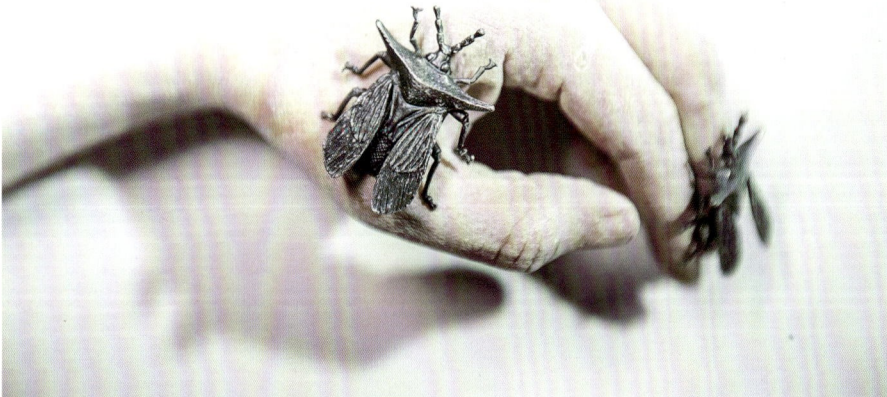

Paula Estrada
Pygoplatys de la sombra
Silver, patina
....
⊙ Juan Fernando Cano

Olga Košica and Rok Mar
Decay
Polyamide
....
Matjaž Banič

Jose Marin
Objetos sin peso
Titanium, yellow sapphires

◎ Miquel Valls

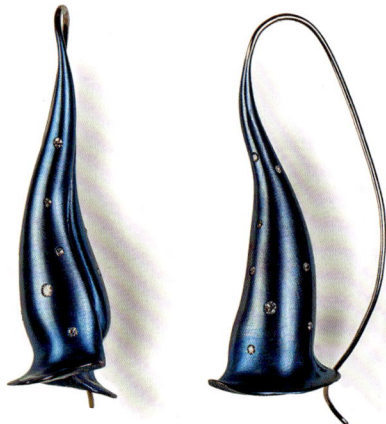

Jose Marin
Cayeron mil chicas
Titanium, diamonds

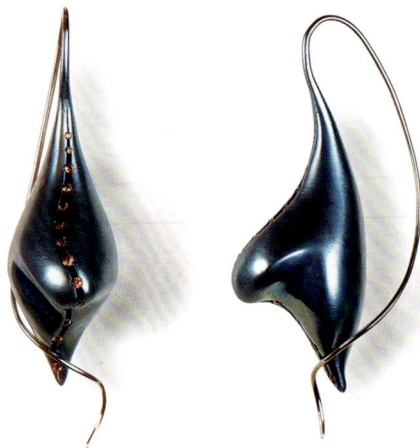

◎ Miquel Valls

Jose Marin
Peach seed
Titanium, diamonds,
peach sapphires

◎ Miquel Valls

Rita Soto Ventura
Pliegues de la Memoria I
Horsehair, vegetable fibre,
Tampico, silver
....
⊙ Juan Gálvez

Kim Yong Joo
From a Red Phoenix
Hook-and-loop fastener,
thread, sterling silver

Myoungwook Huh

Paul Wells
Proxima Earrings
Oxidised sterling silver, 18ct
yellow gold

⊙ Anastasia Young

Paul Wells
Crescent Curl Earrings
Oxidised sterling silver, 18ct
yellow gold

⊙ Anastasia Young

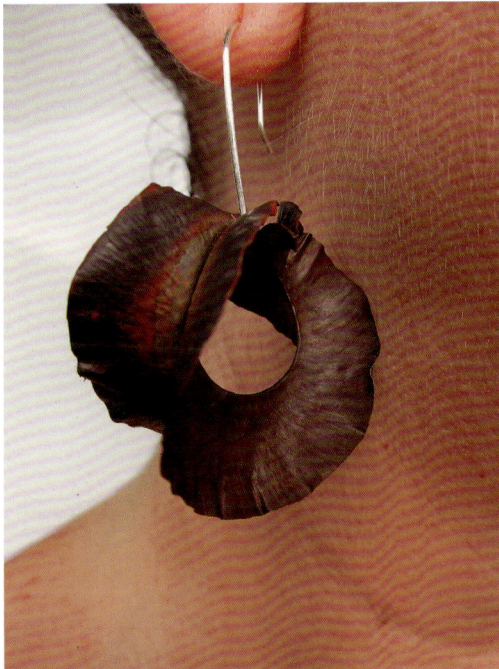

Pepo Raventós
Microcosm
Copper

⊙ Gemma Pinedo

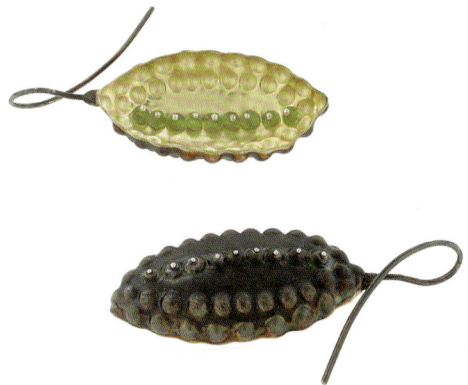

Margo Nelissen
Hidden fruit
(collection Hidden)
Silver, patinated/guilt, peridot

⊙ By the artist

Margo Nelissen
Seed pod on a twig, outside
(collection Hidden)
Silver, gold, carnelian, partly patinated

⊙ By the artist

Andrea Serini
La piel que me habita
Vegetable fibre. American agave,
copper, silver, lacquer, enamels,
vegetable dyes, patinas

⊙ By the artist

Adriana Díaz
Aborigen
930 silver and 18kt gold,
Fairmined materials

⊙ By the artist

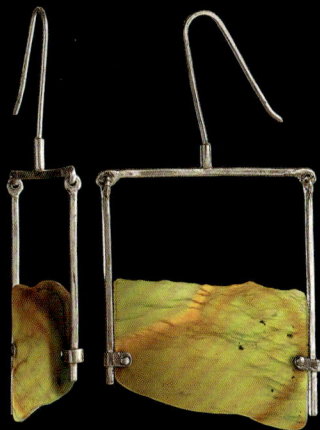

Jacqueline Morren
Golden3
Refurbished 925 silver,
pounamu

....

© Stefan Roberts

Sandra Enterline
Barrel Fringe Earring
Oxidised sterling silver, 18k gold

◎ Mark Johann

Liisa Hashimoto
Chain Chandelier Earring
Silver, brass

◎ Chima

Sandra Enterline
Fringe Earring
Oxidised sterling silver, steel,
24K gold

◎ Mark Johann

Jan Smith
Folded Floral
Sterling silver, pearls
....
◎ Gillean Proctor Photography

Jan Smith
Textured Linear Drops
Sterling silver, pearls
....
◎ Gillean Proctor Photography

Jan Smith
Wrapped Tapered Pods
Sterling silver, copper, vitreous
enamel
....
◎ Gillean Proctor Photography

Judy McCaig
Landscape Points
Silver, 18ct gold, gold leaf,
tombac, herkimer diamond
crystals

⌾ By the artist

Judy McCaig
Shifting Sands
Silver, 18ct gold, gold leaf

⌾ By the artist

Jennie Gill
Diamond Drops
Oxidised silver, 18ct,
uncut diamonds

⌾ Jerry Lampson

Emily Culver
Clamp Set
Stainless steel, wood,
14k yellow gold, silver,
leather, fabric, thread

By the artist

Gayane Avetisyan
Touch has a memory 2
Sterling silver, copper, enamel,
satin
....
◎ Anthony McLean

Gayane Avetisyan
Touch has a memory 3
Sterling silver, copper, enamel,
chiffon
....
◎ Anthony McLean

Namkyung Lee
Beyond the Scene
Sterling silver, photograph
printed on acrylic
....
◎ By the artist

Namkyung Lee
Image Archive
Sterling silver, photograph
printed on acrylic
....
◎ By the artist

Kim Nogueira
Conversations with
the ancestors

Silver, antique tintype, rhodolite
garnets, spinel, south sea pearl,
Tahitian pearl, brown zircon

◎ By the artist

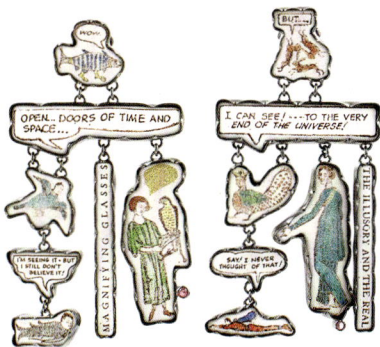

Kim Nogueira
Avalon

Silver, copper, vitreous
enamel, 24k, sapphire

◎ By the artist

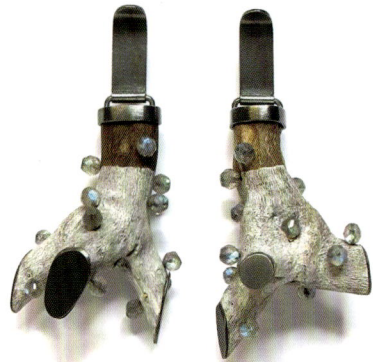

Terhi Tolvanen
Blue Drops
Aquamarine, wood, graphite, paint, silver

◎ By the artist

Terhi Tolvanen
Frosty XL
Heather wood, labradorite, paint, silver

◎ By the artist

Martina Obid Mlakar
Ravenclaw
Silver 925/000, oxidised, citrine

◎ Anton Mlakar

Tobias Andersson
Pearl
Silver, vitreous enamel
....
○ Anna Andersson

Brunella Alfinito
Yozakura – Hana mi!
Shibuichi, gold, pink sapphire,
jade

© Emanuela D'Ambrosi

138

Elif Ustunel
Lovers
Silver, diamonds
....
◎ Mikail Cebeci

Elif Ustunel
Masks
Silver
....
◎ Mikail Cebeci

Susanne Henry
Double Fringe Earrings
Steel, 23k gold, sterling silver

Jocelyn Negron

Susanne Henry
The Fringey Chain Earring
Steel, 24k gold, 23k gold, 14k gold-fill

Jocelyn Negron

Susanne Henry
Extended Full Fringe Earrings
Steel, 24k gold, 23k gold, 14k gold-fill

Jocelyn Negron

Maria Rosa Franzin
Ebony Gold
Silver, pure gold, gold750,
ebony
....
By the artist

Carla Garcia Durlan
Jardín del des(h)echo 2
Acrylic paint on alpaca, silver,
wood and copper

⊙ Luiza la Cava

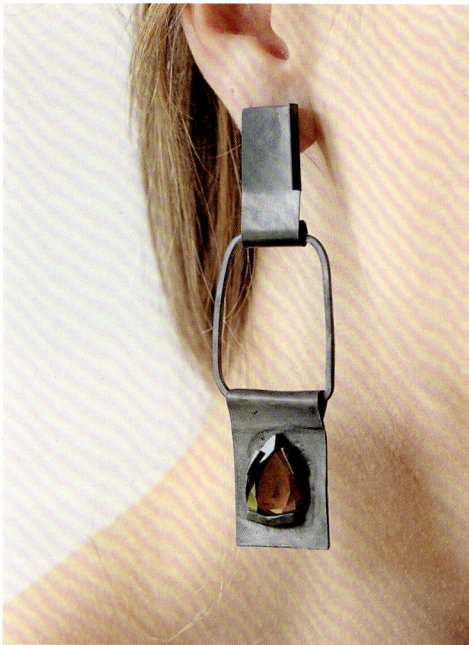

Stefanie Verhoef
Mixed Feelings
Tourmaline Earrings
Oxidised silver, chocolate
brown tourmaline

⊙ Josephine Verhoef

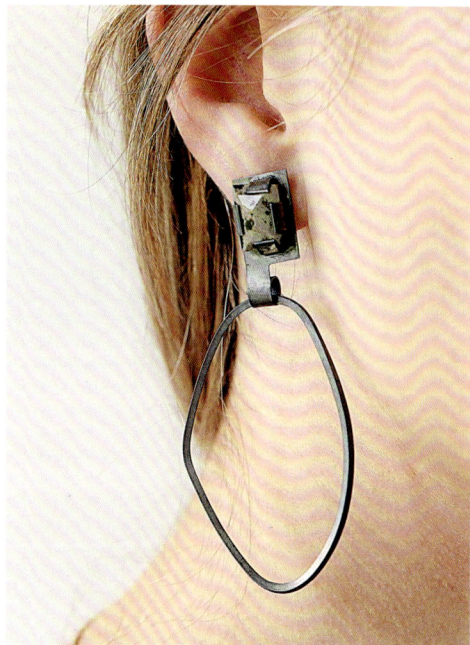

Stefanie Verhoef
Mixed Feelings Uneven
Snippet Pair
Oxidised silver, dalmatian jasper

⊙ Josephine Verhoef

Stefanie Verhoef
Snippet Setting Earrings
Oxidised silver, leopard skin
jasper

⊙ Josephine Verhoef

Stefanie Verhoef
Mixed Feelings Ruby
Zoisite Earrings
Oxidised silver, ruby zoisite

⊙ Josephine Verhoef

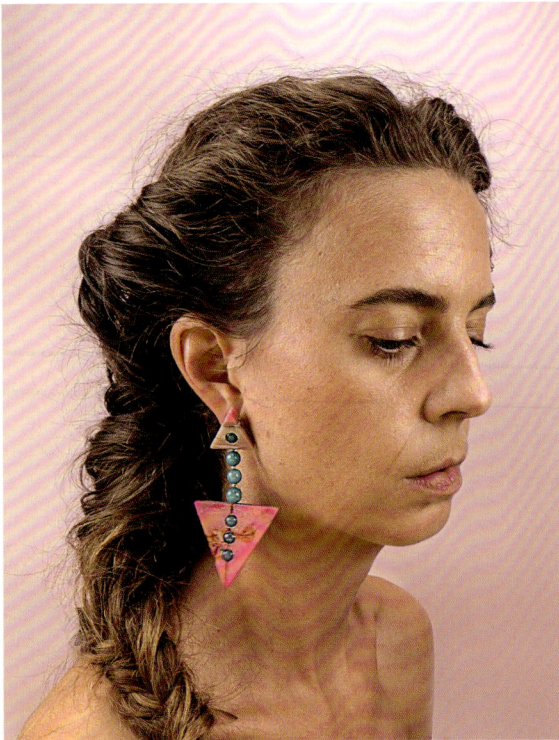

Stephie Morawetz
Plagate I - Pink
Plagate (plastic agate), silver,
coloured agate beads, thread

⌾ By the artist

Stephie Morawetz
Plagate II - Black
Plagate (plastic agate), silver,
coloured rock crystal beads,
thread

⌾ By the artist

Stephie Morawetz
Plagate II - Blue
Plagate (plastic agate), silver,
coloured rock crystal beads,
thread

⌾ By the artist

Stephie Morawetz
Plagate I - Yellow
Plagate (plastic agate), silver,
coloured agate beads, thread
....
By the artist

Cristina Zani
Blue and gold
Gold plated silver, wood,
paint

⊙ By the artist

Cristina Zani
Green and gold
Silver, patina, wood,
paint, gold leaf

⊙ By the artist

Cristina Zani
Grey and gold
Gold plated silver, wood,
paint, gold leaf

⊙ By the artist

Sofia Bankeström
Wood
Juniper wood, gold
....
⊙ By the artist

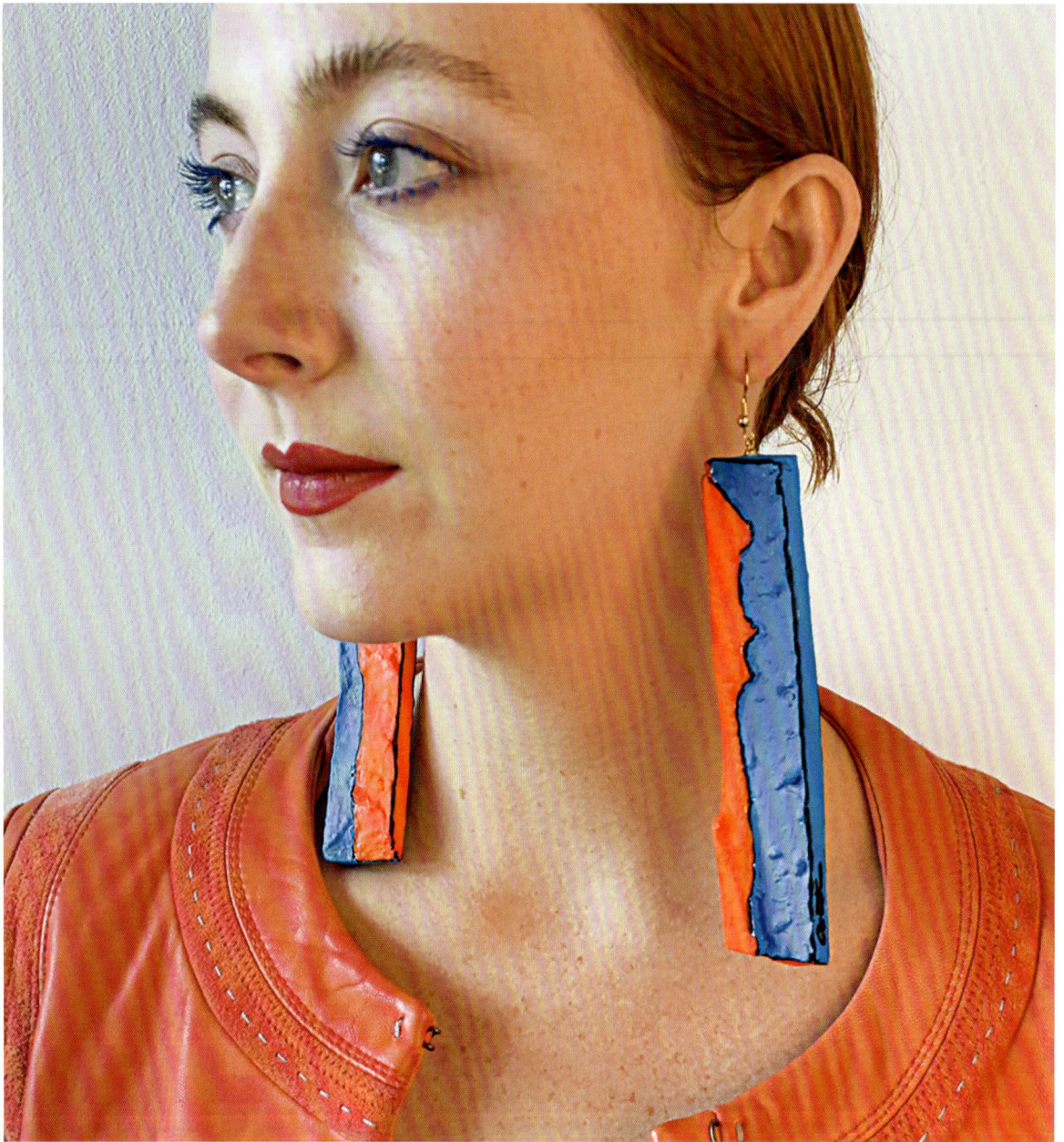

Jim Cotter
Featherweight
Styrofoam, paint, gold
⟡ Anja Korosec

Julia Turner
Blue Shift Earrings
Walnut, gesso, ink, silver
....
◎ By the artist

Julia Turner
Forma Earrings
Walnut, maple, silver
....
◎ By the artist

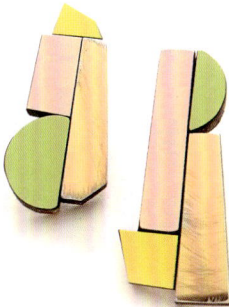

Karen Vanmol
Koloro Gemo
Wood, laminate, silver
....
◎ By the artist

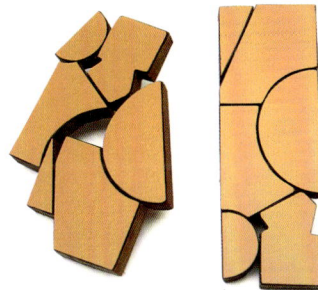

Karen Vanmol
AKA#Iseefaces
Wood, laminate, silver
....
◎ By the artist

SOPHISTICATED

Räthel & Wolf
ANN Ear Cuff
Silver plated brass

Valerie Schmidt

Ángela María Muñoz Correa
Pendientes Cascadas
Sterling silver 925

Alex Arenas

Nóra Tengely
Present continuous
series_Silver earrings
Silver 925

◎ Baptiste Coulon

Ellen Cohen
Asymetrical Opal Hollow
Form Earrings
Sterling silver, opals, 18K gold,
18K gold bimetal, 14K gold
posts

⌖ Cole Roger / Cole Image

Ellen Cohen
Turquoise Hollow Form
Earrings
Sterling silver, turquoise,
18K gold bimetal

⌖ Mark Visbal Photography

Natalie Hoogeveen
Lemon quartz with green
enamel
Silver, gold, enamel with photo
transfer, lemon quartz

⌖ Erwin Maes

Natalie Hoogeveen
Green enamelled leaves
Silver, enamel, diamonds,
prasolite

⌖ Erwin Maes

Diana Greenwood
Forget Me Not Earrings
Silver, 18ct gold, sapphires
....
◎ Paul Mounsey

Diana Greenwood
Summer Garden Charm
Earrings
Sterling silver, 18ct gold, faceted
sapphire, Peruvian opal and ruby
beads
....
◎ Paul Mounsey

Kristina Laass
Aphrodite
White gold, D-coloured
diamonds, South Sea white
pearls
....
◎ Dmytro Las

Kristina Laass
Aquamarine Dawn
White gold, aquamarines
in a fancy cut with bubbles,
pink sapphires inlaid under
and around aquamarines
....
◎ Hnat Burma

Lluís Comín
Cubs
Silver, 18k yellow gold

◎ By the artist

Lluís Comín
Cubs
Silver, 18k yellow gold

◎ By the artist

Arata Fuchi
Stillness 9
Silver, oxidised silver powder,
pure gold, pearls, shibuichi

◎ By the artist

Arata Fuchi
Stillness 15
Silver, oxidised silver powder,
pure gold, pearls, shibuichi,
oxidised pure silver

◎ By the artist

Youjin Um
Hexagonal object I
& overlay structure I
Silver

⊙ Kwangchoon Park

Jenny Reeves
Quartz Lazulite Hex Drop
Silver, smoky quartz, lazulite,
rhodolite garnet

By the artist

Lucy Martin
Jali Earrings (Pinkgreens)
Tourmaline, rhodolite garnet, peridot,
tsavorite garnet, pink amethyst,
oxidised silver, 18ct gold.

Jeremy Johns

Liaung Chung
A View from Above
earrings #12
18 yellow gold, tourmaline,
diamonds

Shu Ching Yang

Mark Nuell
Asymmetric Blue Sapphire Drop
Earrings
Freeform Australian blue sapphires
weighing 3.26cts, 18ct yellow gold

Karen Bengall

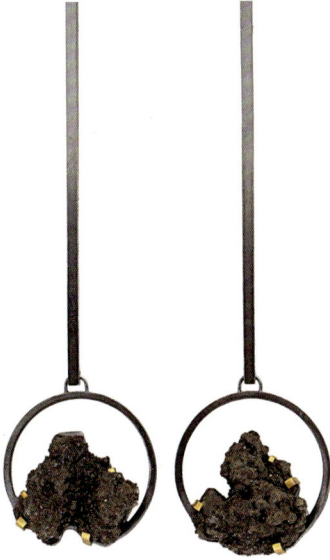

Kate Eickelberg
Steel splatter circle
Steel, gold, silver, patina

By the artist

Kate Eickelberg
Teardrop steel splatter
Steel, gold, silver, patina

By the artist

Jenny Reeves
Aqua Tourmaline Circle Drops
Silver, gold, aquamarine, green tourmaline

By the artist

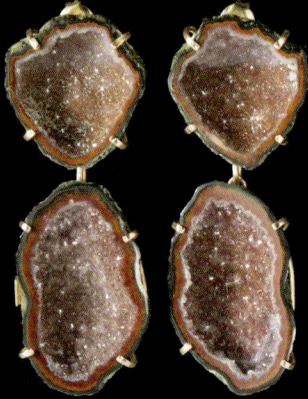

Nicolas Estrada
Tabasco
Gold, drusen
....
◎ Joan Soto

Nicolas Estrada
Rosa con limón
Gold, rock crystal, lemon
citrine
....
◎ Joan Soto

Heather Guidero
Dendritic Agate Earrings
18k gold, dendritic agate,
12 tcw diamonds
....
◎ Cole Rodger

Heather Guidero
Carved Prong Set
Tourmalated Quartz
Earrings
Oxidised and bright
sterling silver, 18k gold,
tourmalated quartz
....
◎ Cole Rodger

Heather Guidero
Wyoming Jade Earrings
18k gold, surface cut
Wyoming jade
....
◎ Cole Rodger

Danielle Cadef
Arie (Arielah) Earrings
Silver, carved capiz shell, silk

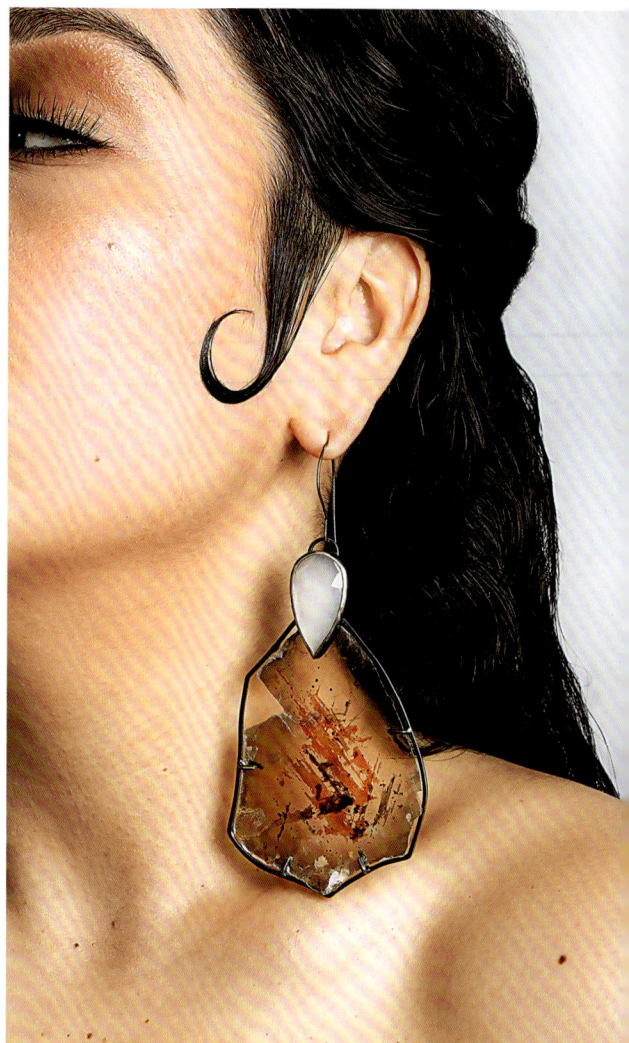

◉ Antonia Tapia

Danielle Cadef
Moonstone Red Mica
Earrings
Silver, mica, white moonstone

◉ Antonia Tapia

Biba Schutz
1-MIN-40
Sterling silver, tourmaline,
Mexican opal and ruby
....
◎ Ron Boszko

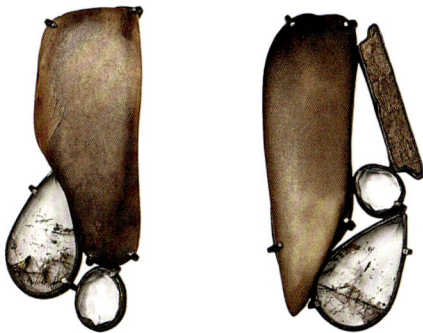

Robert Thomas Mullen
Bone Clusters
Fossilized walrus tusk,
mammoth tusk, rutilated
quartz, quartz and silver
....
◎ By the artist

Robert Thomas Mullen
Large Wreath Dangles
Petrified wood, petroleum
quartz, rutilated quartz, rock
crystal and silver
....
◎ By the artist

Alma Sophia Grønli Geller
Equinox
Silver, black rhodium, blue topaz,
quartz, citrine

◎ Julia Skupny

Alma Sophia Grønli Geller
Dark side of the moon
Silver, black rhodium, grey
moonstone, white sapphires

◎ Julia Skupny

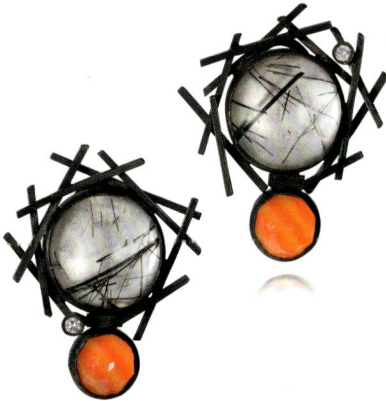

Daphne Krinos
Nest Earrings
Oxidised silver, tourmaline quartz,
carnelians, diamonds

◎ Juliet Sheath

Daphne Krinos
Suspended Earrings
Oxidised silver, green amethysts,
diamonds

◎ Juliet Sheath

Nicolas Estrada
5 colores
Gold, rubies, amethysts,
citrines, tourmaline quartz

Irene Mykal

Rachel Quinn
Onyx cupid's heart
Gold, onyx, diamonds,
rubies

◎ Wolf Gottlieb

Rachel Quinn
Royal skull
Gold, silver, diamonds,
rubies, pearls

◎ Wolf Gottlieb

Rachel Quinn
Monsoon
Gold, keshi pearls, white topaz

◎ Diamond Graphic Studios

Helena Romanova
Cor
Stainless steel

⊙ Yurii Romanov

Eszter Sára Kocsor
Black Mirror Earring
Black PVD (Physical Vapor
Deposition) coated stainless
steel, London blue topaz

◎ Marcell Piti

Eszter Sára Kocsor
Black Mirror Earring
Black PVD (Physical Vapor
Deposition) coated stainless
steel, Blue zirconia

◎ Marcell Piti

Christa Lühtje
No title
Gold, garnet

◎ Eva Jünger

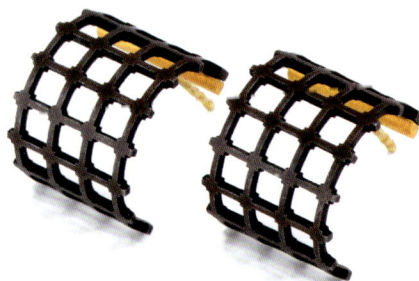

Christa Lühtje
No title
Iron

◎ Eva Jünger

Kate Eickelberg
Nail Head Earrings
Antique (1790s-1820s) square
iron nail heads, 18k gold
....
◎ By the artist

Marta Coderque
Barbados
Gold plated silver with texture,
onyx
....
◎ Maria Granda

Mengnan Zi
Cocoon Collection
Thread, silver, liang fabric

◉ Zhanpin Sheng

Mengnan Zi
Cocoon Collection
Thread, silver, liang fabric

© Zhanpin Sheng

Petra Class Studio
Green Tourmaline Cluster (E5)
Faceted and rose cut green tourmalines,
22K gold bezel, 18K gold

◎ Hap Sakwa

Petra Class Studio
Aquamarine, Sapphire,
Diamond & Pearl Star (EM)
Rough and faceted aquamarines,
yellow and blue sapphires, round
pearl, rose cut diamond, 22K gold
bezel, 18K gold

◎ Hap Sakwa

Michele A. Friedman
Hex Earrings
Oxidised sterling silver
with wool felt

◎ Cole Rodger

Michele A. Friedman
Memphis Earrings
Oxidised sterling with wool felt

◎ Cole Rodger

Rike Bartels
Helios
Gold, turmaline, pearls
....
⊙ Jens Mauritz

Rike Bartels
Voodoo
Gold, amber, coral, pearls
....
⊙ Jens Mauritz

Rike Bartels
Little owl
Gold
....
⊙ Jens Mauritz

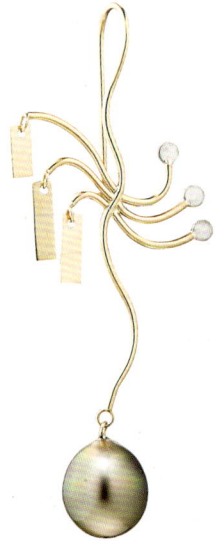

Saskia Besiakov
Playground
Gold, pearl, garnet

◎ James Bates

Saskia Besiakov
Dancing bird
Gold, silver, pearl

◎ James Bates

Saskia Besiakov
Japan
Gold, silver, patina, corals

◎ James Bates

Mengnan Zi
Freedom Collection
Copper, Silver

◎ Pengfei Xu

Zhuyun Chen
Electric Wave Earrings
Silver, topaz

Tsz Lo

Zhuyun Chen
Moiré Motion Earrings
Silver, topaz

Tsz Lo

Casey Newberg
GamGam's Favorite
Earrings – Pink
Readymade earring,
powdercoated and laser etched
aluminum jacket, stainless
findings

By the artist

Casey Newberg
GamGam's Favorite
Earrings – Green
Readymade earring,
powdercoated and laser
etched aluminum jacket,
stainless findings

By the artist

Casey Newberg
"Diamond Heirloom" –
Now on Sale!
Readymade earring,
powdercoated and laser etched
aluminum jacket, stainless
findings

By the artist

Tala Yuan
Personification-2
Pearls, aventurine, silver
⦿ By the artist

Tala Yuan
Evening glow
Baroque pearls, freshwater
pearl, silver oxide

⦿ By the artist

Angela Bubash
Fin #55
Sterling silver

◎ By the artist

Angela Bubash
Fin #54
Sterling silver,
green chalcedony

◎ By the artist

Angela Bubash
Fin #56
Sterling silver

◎ By the artist

Edna Milevsky
Spirograph Hoop
Earrings

Sterling silver, cultured pearls,
natural sapphires

⟲ Digital By Design,
Paul Ambtman

Edna Milevsky
Pearl Slider Mismatched
Earrings

Sterling silver, cultured pearls

⟲ Digital By Design,
Paul Ambtman

Florian Wagner
Longing for...
Mother of pearl, steel,
gold, Tahitian pearls

Jürgen Knoth

Räthel & Wolf
Selma
Silver plated brass

○ Valerie Schmidt

Räthel & Wolf
Dominik
Silver plated brass

◎ Valerie Schmidt

EXHUBERANT

Xiao Han Zhang
Ray
Brass, thread, pearl

Dlany

Vania Ruiz
Periander Butterfly
Epoxy resin, varnish, ink,
sterling silver

Mario Medina

Vania Ruiz
European Peacock
Butterfly
Epoxy resin, varnish, ink,
sterling silver

Pablo Marcos

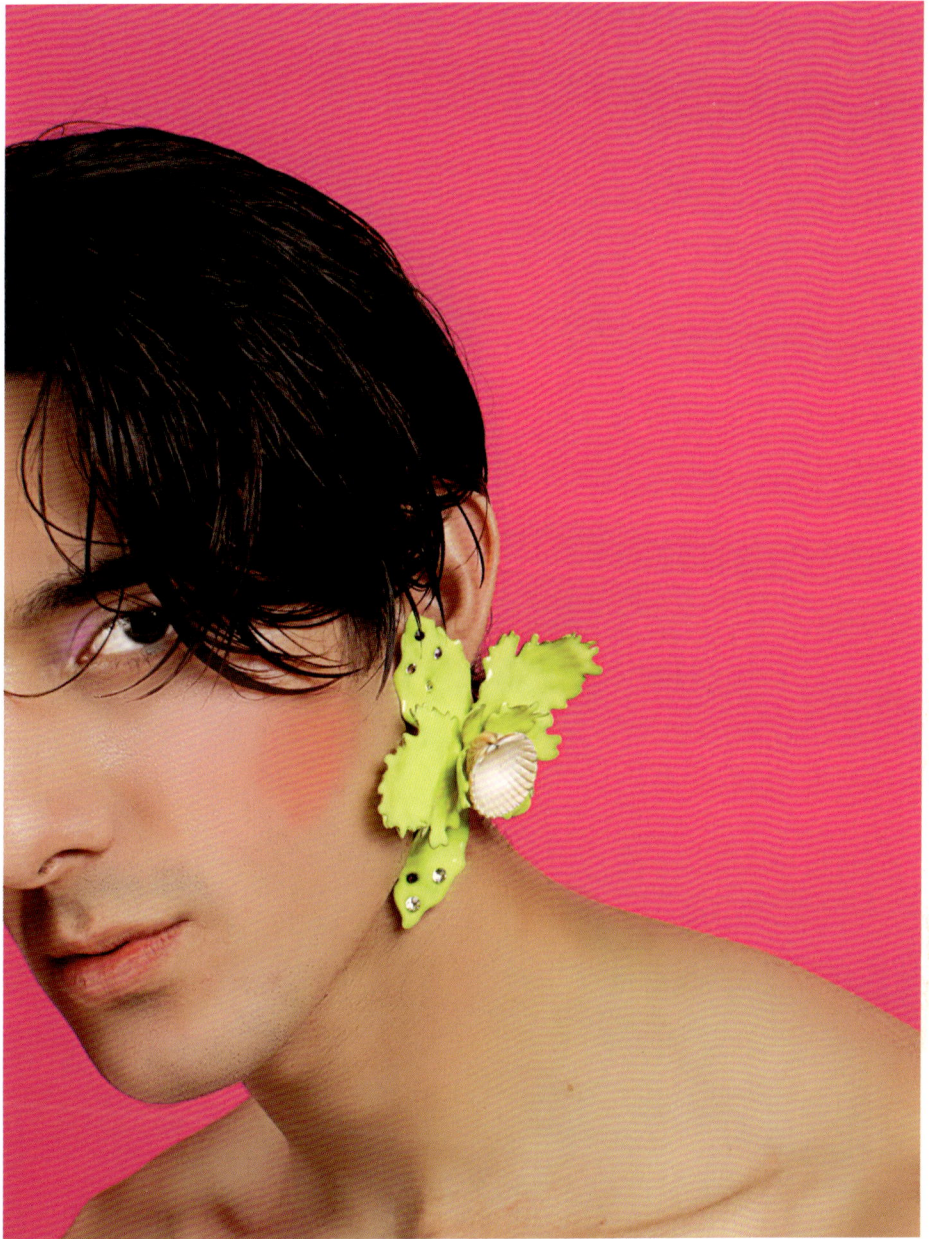

Fernando Haro
Gender Bloom
Enamelled brass, zirconia
and sea shells
....
◎ Nieves Alonso

Jeffrey Lloyd Dever
Petal Blue
Polymer clay, stainless steel
cable, sterling silver

······································
◎ Gregory R. Staley

Jeffrey Lloyd Dever
Summer Blossom
Polymer clay, sterling silver,
stainless steel cable

······································
◎ Gregory R. Staley

Jeffrey Lloyd Dever
Eves Retreat
Polymer clay, sterling silver,
glass pins

······································
◎ Gregory R. Staley

Heejoo Kim
Green Study
Enameled copper, sterling silver

◎ Junghoon Oh

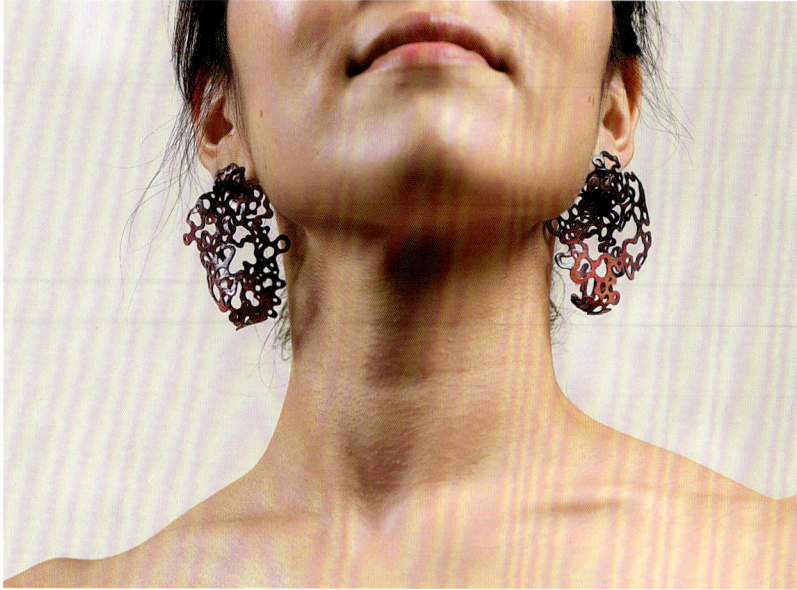

Cassandra Prinzi
Dolce Mare Earrings
Copper, powder coating, enamel
paint, sterling silver

Francesco Vicenzi

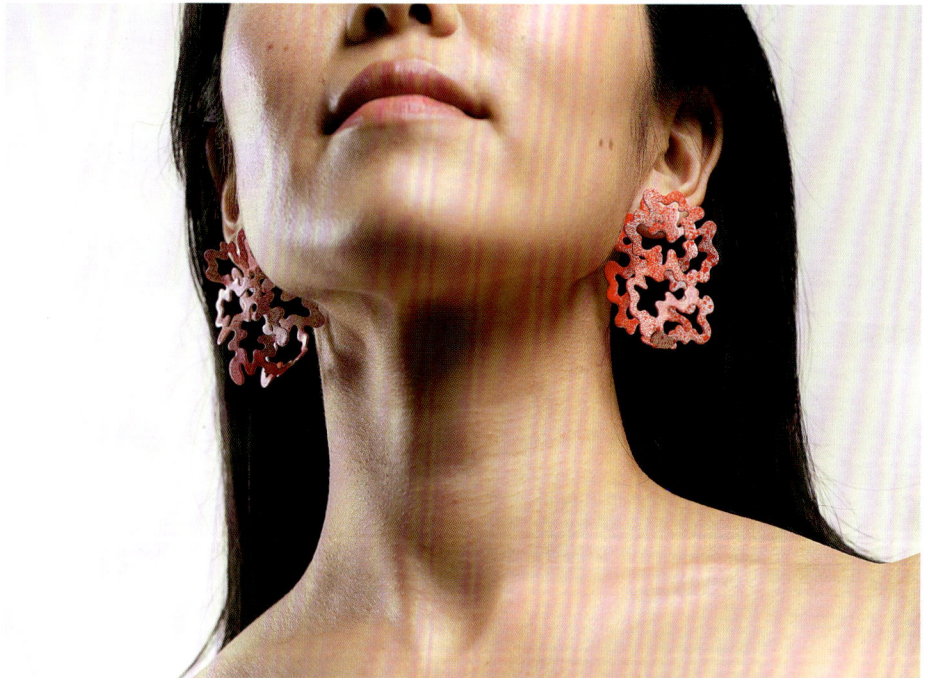

Cassandra Prinzi
Clamshell Earrings
Copper, powder coating, enamel
paint, sterling silver

Francesco Vicenzi

Heng Lee
Auspicious Cloud III
Nickle silver plated with
platinum, thread, silk organza

◎ By the artist

Sandra Roldan
Impacto
Crochet technique, filigree,
925 silver, crystal and bead
embroidery.

◎ Sergio Ramírez

Sandra Roldan
Profanación
Tatting technique, filigree,
925 silver, gold plating, crystal
embroidery

◎ Sergio Ramírez

Atelier Iris Nijenhuis
The Diamond - Aquarelle
Laser cut puzzle pieces
of artificial suede, silver pin

⊙ Floris Nijensikkens

Zhanna Assanova
Kurak earrings
A zip

© Zhenya Volkova

Sofia Jaramillo
Bocanegra
Glass beads and wax thread

⦾ Sebastián Castaño Ospina

Helena Romanova
Enigma
Sequins, paper, stainless steel

◎ Yurii Romanov

Helena Romanova
Omolade
Wood, stainless steel

Yurii Romanov

Helena Romanova
Amanda
Rhinestone chain,
stainless steel, coating

⊙ Yurii Romanov

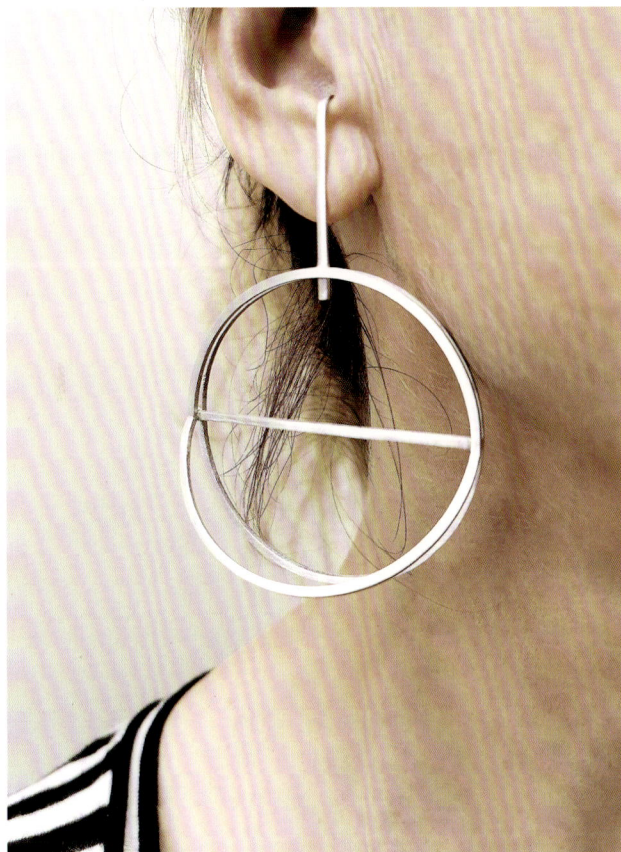

Eugènia Arnavat
Cicle lunar
Silver

◎ By the artist

Maren Düsel
Circleline Creoles
Selective laser sintering:
nylon, sterling silver

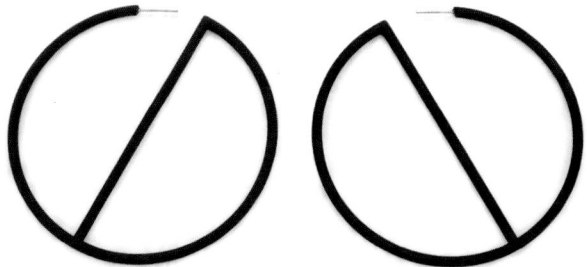

Christin Snyders

Sogand Nobahar
Black Lolita
Sintered nylon powder, silver

Taimaz Ashtari

Helena Romanova
Anita
Sequins, stainless steel

◎ Yurii Romanov

Patricia Mogni
Apacheta
Sintered nylon powder,
silver

⊙ By the artist

Lavinia Rossetti
Nidi3
Silver

MILL Photo Studio

Brunella Alfinito
Fireworks (Oenothera Fruticosa)-
Qualcosa di rosso
Gold, shibuichi, smoky quartz, spinel, carnelian

Emanuela D'Ambrosi

Yojae Lee
Spider
Silver, brass,
mixed material

◎ Choon Kwang Park

Yojae Lee
Water stick insect
Silver, brass,
mixed material

© Choon Kwang Park

Clara del Papa
Árbol de la vida

925 silver pickle, natural
patina, balsamic vinegar,
24kt gold

◎ Emmanuela Gasparella

Leticia Llera
Sprout
Tumbaga, copper with patina

◎ Joaquín Mario López Sánchez

INDEX OF ARTISTS

Adriana Díaz — COLOMBIA

/ adrianadiazhiguera@gmail.com
/ www.adrianadiazh.com

"I studied industrial design, silversmithing and jewellery arts in Bogota and Barcelona. My pieces are the fruit of experimenting with different techniques seeking texture, folds, colours, and possibilities in metal. Some of the pieces I make have clean, subtle, timeless forms and are inspired by geometry, repetition, and sculpture, while others are the result of a more personal search among metaphors such as the passage of time, decay, and the warp. I'm interested in the ethical origin of materials, and I promote responsible jewellery initiatives. I'm always searching for more sustainable processes."

Alma Sophia Grønli Geller — USA/NORWAY

/ mail@almasophiadesign.com
/ www.almasophia.com

Alma Sophia is a Norwegian goldsmith and jewellery designer/maker based in London since 2013. She makes her jewellery from her studio space at Cockpit Arts in Bloomsbury. Sculptural form is central to her designs. Alma uses square tube that she cuts and combines in different ways, and repeated shapes create distinctive forms and new wholes, ensuring that every piece is unique. She holds a First-Class Honours degree in Silversmithing, Goldsmithing and Jewellery from the University for the Creative Arts, Rochester and achieved her Journeyman's certificate in goldsmithing from Plus School, Norway in 2010.

Ana Cardim — PORTUGAL

/ contact@anacardim-jewellery.com
/ https://anacardim-jewellery.com

Ana Cardim expressed, from an early age, her desire to create jewellery that transcends the borders of mere body adornment. With a degree in Art History, she has a Master's in Theory and Aesthetics of Contemporary Arts from the University of Barcelona and coupled with solid parallel training in the jewellery field. In the scope of author jewellery, she developed an original critical discourse that was recognized through institutional support and prizes. As a jewellery designer, she highlights the most aesthetic aspect of her creations, having won several design awards. Her designs follow sophisticated criteria of lightness and formal debugging and opt for an asymmetrical geometry that refers to a temporality that crosses the classic imaginary and futuristic innovation.

Ana Pina — PORTUGAL

/ atelier@anapina.com / www.anapina.com

Ana Pina was born in 1980, in Porto, Portugal. She graduated with a degree in architecture (FAUP, 2004) and worked in an office for a few years, until she found her passion for contemporary jewellery. Her background in this area includes a professional course at the school Engenho e Arte, in addition to complementary workshops.

She has developed her own jewellery brand since 2012, and opened Tincal lab in 2015, a workshop and gallery space that aims to promote this creative area through collaborations, workshops, and exhibitions. Ana creates jewels with a strong abstract, minimalist and geometric inspiration. Each collection combines elements of a common vocabulary in a game of geometric relations and asymmetries, as if they were letters building words inserted in a bigger text.

Andrea Auer — AUSTRIA

/ buero@andreaauer.at / www.andreaauer.at

Born in 1972, Andrea Auer completed her training as a belt-maker, goldsmith and silversmith at HTL Steyr in Austria and holds a degree from the University of Art and Design in Linz (Austria). Since graduating in 2002 she has been based in Vienna, working as an independent artist. Her work has been exhibited nationally and internationally, including at MAK - Museum of Applied Arts in Vienna, Pforzheim Jewellery Museum, Centre d'Art Santa Mònica in Barcelona, and Première Classe in Paris. In 2019 she was selected for Schmuck 2019 in Munich. Andrea Auer was awarded Artist Residencies in Austria, China, Czech Republic, Estonia, and the Netherlands. Her work is held in permanent collections including Municipal City of Linz, Museum Espace Solidor in Cagnes-Sur-Mer, and Shanghai Art Collection Museum.

Andrea Serini — ARGENTINA

/ aniserini@yahoo.com.ar / @a.s_andreaserini

"I think jewellery accentuates or complements the verbal and non-verbal communication of the human body. The body speaks, announces, describes, predicts. The destiny of a ring could be accompanying the hand in the tender gesture of a caress. The fate of an earring perhaps is to join the ear in receiving the sounds emitted by words, music, and nature. I always imagine a brooch listening to the durability of life, the inaudible beating of the heart that hides nearby, behind."

Andrea Vaggione — ARGENTINA

/ contact@andreavaggione.com
/ www.andreavaggione.com

"As Argentine artist and designer, I discovered the world of contemporary jewellery in Córdoba, my hometown, in 2001. In 2005 I moved to Barcelona, where I learned welding techniques at the El Taller de Joyería school. In 2012 I moved to Lyon, where I won the 'Talents de mode' contest, which allowed me to open my studio-shop in the Village de Créateurs. Currently, I live in the south of France and in addition to jewellery, I've begun to explore other expressive mediums. My work revolves around notions of permanent transformation, perpetual motion, birth, rebirth, and migration."

Angela Bubash — USA

/ angelabubash@gmail.com
/ www.angelabubash.com

"I am a studio jeweler and educator residing in Rice VA where I currently teach at Longwood University and maintain my own studio practice. I attained a BFA from Edinboro University of Pennsylvania and an MFA from Southern Illinois University Carbondale. Other accomplishments include completing the residency at Penland School of Crafts in North Carolina and exhibiting my work nationally and internationally.
Silver and nylon fins in various sizes and configurations provide a sense of motion and flux in direct contrast to specimens captured in glass and cotton. Shadows are cast and move with time or presentation of the work. Light pools, reflects, and highlights. All the while, crafted domes of color offer a moment of pause amidst a dynamic, moving environment."

Ángela María Muñoz Correa — COLOMBIA

/ contacto.atalea@gmail.com / @atalea.co

"Since I was a little girl, I liked to experiment with materials, and my hands were my first tools to create. Cutting, gluing, and painting I managed to materialize small objects that I wore with pride. Ten years ago, this interest made me discover jewellery while studying Industrial Design. Transforming metal and shaping it with the help of a few tools was what captivated me the most. This was the beginning of a passion that was fuelled by curiosity, teachers and learning, and the joy of those who received and wore a piece of jewellery made by me."

Anja Berg — CHILE

/ aniberg@gmail.com

"I grew up in tune with jewellery. Since I was 15, I've been involved with this profession, which I studied with different masters in Chile and Spain and at the Alchimia School in Italy. My interest in making jewellery is to narrate through it. Not only to beautify but to achieve a visual and tangible poetry, delving into the relationship between the material and its forms, to continue conveying on the body symbolism and meaning. This set of stone earrings is part of that search."

Anna Rafecas — SPAIN
/ laboratoriidees@gmail.com / @annarafecas_
Jewellery maker, enameller, and coordinator of the jewellery department at the Arsenal school. Professional artisan master specialising in fired enamel and jewellery.
She has been awarded and selected at national and international events, galleries, museums, and private collections. Jewellery as personal identity and communicative artifact, exploring through passion symbols inherent to the creative process. The search for a balance between imperfection, beauty and profundity found in nature. Growth, learning, doubt, decadence, and death. Beginning and end process.

Anna Vlahos — AUSTRALIA
/ hello@annavlahos.com / www.annavlahos.com
Anna Vlahos is an Australian jewellery artist, currently based in Athens, Greece. She received a Bachelor of Arts (Visual Arts) Honours from Edith Cowan University in Perth, Western Australia, in 2002, majoring in printmaking. She then received a Certificate IV in Jewellery Design and Manufacture. In 2007 she moved to Athens, Greece and since then has been working as a studio jeweller, her work being shown in exhibitions in Europe and abroad. Anna's work stems from an interest in pattern making in both the ancient and natural worlds, drawing from her history in two-dimensional printmaking. Inspiration is taken from the rich history of surface design of ancient Greece and beyond, using this to rebuild a new nature from memories and histories.

Anne Bader — GERMANY
/ auri.info@googlemail.com
/ www.auri-jewellery.com
Anne Bader trained as a goldsmith at Staatliche Zeichenakademie Hanau. "Inspired by the traditional Japanese art of origami, I create abstract structures that join volumes and lightness in an expressive form. I am fascinated by how reduced and simplified shapes can generate a powerful appearance. Bringing together the contrasts of light paper and heavy, rigid metal through applying an origami pattern by folding the silver or gold sheet gives rise to an exciting tension. As the shape appears delicate and light like paper, I try to render the work process as simple and logical as possible, such as using cold connection techniques instead of soldering."

Annie Tung — CANADA
/ hello@annietungcreative.com
/ annietungcreative.com
Toronto-based jewellery artist-designer Annie Tung has been working with jewellery since 2007. She creates jewellery and objects from a craft and design perspective. Annie received her undergraduate degree from OCAD University's Material Art and Design program, with a focus on Jewellery/Metalsmithing (2007), followed by an artist-residency at Harbourfront Centre (2007–10). She graduated from the École cantonale d'art de Lausanne MAS Luxe programme in Switzerland (2015). Annie is currently Assistant Professor at OCAD University where she teaches jewellery and digital design in the Material Art & Design programme.

Arata Fuchi — JAPAN
/ info@arata-fuchi.com / www.arata-fuchi.com
"Japanese find beauty in everyday life, for example, in seasonal change and natural phenomenon, and believe that God exists in all these things. This is the basic thinking of Shinto. My work is inspired by the Japanese sense of beauty, that is 'beauty of form that nature not artifice creates', and the 'vitality of nature'. Many inspirations arrive from nature. To express these, I developed the ancient technique of South Korea called Keum-Boo in my own way. From trial and error, I created an original technique I call pulverization. For this technique, the surface is covered with silver (metal) powder to make the surfaces rough and irregular. With this irregular shadow a peculiar feeling is expressible."

Ariadne Kapelioti — GREECE
/ hello@ariadnekapelioti.com
/ www.ariadnekapelioti.com
Born in Greece, Ariadne Kapelioti is a jewellery designer who trained as a physicist, a metalsmith, and an architect in Thessaloniki and London. She creates contemporary jewellery in a conscious way, built on the concept of eternity and optimism as a strategy for making a brighter future.
Her current work, the "Phaos" jewellery collection, draws inspiration from the nature of light as the core of everyday life, which laid the foundations for modern physics and the Information Age. In addition, through the story of light, project "Phaos" pays tribute to all the pioneers, those radically successful people who have a ferocious drive that makes them never give up. "Phaos" (φάος/φως) is the ancient Greek word for light.

B

Barbara Klar, Clear Metals, Inc. — USA
/ barbara@clearmetals.com
/ www.barbaraklar.com
After graduating from the Cleveland Institute of Art in 1979, Barbara opened her first standalone store, Clear Metals, in NYC's East Village during the mid80's. In 1991 she moved the store into the fashion and shopping Mecca that is SoHo, where it was located for ten years until Barbara relocated her life and studio upstate to the Hudson Valley. She continues to grow her business, her wholesale line, and her special commissions. Clear Metals is a testament to Barbara's fascinating collection, a unique presentation of one-of-a kind and limited-edition gold and silver jewellery, completely designed and crafted by her in her upstate studios.

Beate Pfefferkorn — GERMANY
/ info@elementarisbypfefferkorn.de
/ www.elementarisbypfefferkorn.de
"I received my degree in ceramics from Burg Giebichenstein University in Halle, Germany, where I started my career as a jewellery artist. In the last 10 years I've shown my work at different fairs and exhibitions all around the world and have also won different awards (the most important: in 2021 the German design award, in 2016 the Emerging Artist Award-Fuping/China). The specific characteristics of the material are of great importance. At the beginning of the work process porcelain is a malleable mass and allows highly delicate handling, which is continued by firing it at 1250 °C. The material is not only lovely and beautiful but also very comfortable to wear. The colours of the single pieces vary: vivid tones are placed equally next to virgin white."

Berta Sumpsi — SPAIN
/ berta.nivulat@gmail.com
/ www.bertasumpsi.com
"Designs emerge from one day to the next in my normal life. Certain elements, materials or questions grab my attention. When the sensation lasts, I think there's a concept I want to work with. I want my pieces to communicate through an elemental language and minimal gestures. To play with form or the material, or to mull over a single concept. Things seen up close, and a little obsessively, acquire depth and offer numerous possibilities. I'm content with a few meaningful things."

Thinking, creating, and having one or several elements with which to say something. And for this message to endure when someone wears a piece of jewellery."

Biba Schutz — USA
/ bibaschutz@gmail.com / www.bibaschutz.com
Biba Schutz is a self-taught studio jeweller residing in New York City. Interpreting her observations and experiences, she creates jewellery that teases the senses. Her urban environment encourages her use of space, light, shadow, and materials to create wearable jewellery. Often there are places to hide and travel within the work. A residency at the Corning Museum of Glass was inspirational in creating a body of work that brought additional museum acquisitions as well as Schmuck 2016 to her resume. Her jewellery is in the collections of the Museum of Fine Arts of Boston, the Newark Museum, the Corning Museum of Glass, the Racine Museum of Art, the Dallas Museum of Art, and the Renwick Gallery at the Smithsonian Museum of Art.

Brunella Alfinito — ITALY
/ brunella.alfinito@gmail.com
/ https://brunellalfinito.it
Brunella holds a master's degree in architecture from La Sapienza (Rome), a BFA from Alchimia (Florence), an exchange experience in the 3D Fine Arts Master's Program at MassArt (Boston) and a teaching assistant position in the "Intermediate Jewellery" course at MassArt (Boston). She completed a designer internship at Embr Labs (MIT). Currently, she's working as an independent jewellery artist and is teaching at IED Moda Milan. "Unusual, changeable, illusory. Each material's nature will show to me endless possibilities. Research and experimentation are essential for a coherent elaboration of the thought. Shapes, patinas, textures, surfaces, and colours to express a concept in a close dialogue with the body."

Burcu Sülek — TURKEY
/ Burcu@burcusulek.com / www.burcusulek.com
Born and based in Istanbul, Burcu Sülek is a Turkish designer and maker focused on contemporary jewellery. Just after graduating from the Istanbul Technical University Management Engineering Department, she joined and worked for global brands of consumer electronics as Marketing Manager for over 13 years, until she had the chance to take her whole career in a completely different direction.
Since 2012 she has been enjoying this newfound freedom to express herself through her own jewellery line. Contemporary jewellery makes this freedom more complete by granting her infinite flexibility to create whatever she desires.

C

Cappy Counard — US
/ www.cappycounard.com
"Forged holes that stretch and diminish speak about effort and change. Seams cut apart, and then reassembled are left with a raised line that is reminiscent of stitching, a visible repair. These pieces are about fragility and fallibility, and how essential careful attention is to preserving and creating connection."
Cappy Counard studied Jewelry and Metals at Southern Illinois University at Carbondale where she earned her MFA in 1999. Since then, she has lived in Edinboro, PA where she is a professor at Pennsylvania Western University and makes work in her home studio. Her metalwork is published in many books and has been included in both national and international exhibitions.

Carla Garcia Durlan — SPAIN
/ carlagarciadurlan@gmail.com
/ carlagarciaduran.com
She entered the creative world in 2005 through graphic design at BAU university, in Barcelona, although she always had an evident passion for painting, illustration and objects. A series

of coincidences led her to discover jewellery, and in 2011 she completed the Certificate of Higher Education. Since then, she has completed intensive courses and workshops in the Taller Perill, the School of Arts and Crafts, Escola Visions, and the Massana School. In 2012 she joined the group Joyas Sensacionales (Sensational Jewellery) and in 2013 along with jewellery makers Maria Diez, Sandra Llusà and Clara Niubò, founded the project "Quars d'una", a jewellery collective and distribution platform. In 2018 she was selected in the Herbert-Hofmann, Schmuck Awards 2018 in Germany. And in 2020 she was a finalist in the "Loewe foundation craft prize 2020-2021".

Carmen López — SPAIN
/ carmenlopez.7@gmail.com
/ www.carmenlopezenamel.com
Ceramic and enamel teacher at the schools of Art and Design in Huelva and Seville (Spain). "I am currently immersing myself in the world of contemporary jewellery, mixing enamel, recycled plastic with silver. My pieces are often shown in various exhibition spaces in Spain, Italy, France, Belgium, Germany, Portugal, and Ireland. My work revolves around the conceptual world. My traveling companion is a spoon. Metals, enamels, and recycled plastics are my allies. I want my jewellery to carry a secret code that only the spoon and I know. My passions are teaching and working in my studio."

Caroline Lindholm — SWEDEN
/ caroline@cali.se / www.cali.se
"I received an MFA from Konstfack, National College of Arts, Crafts and Design, Stockholm in 1996. Since then, I have worked in metal making a lot of unique jewellery and silver hollowware for my clients. I love silver and gold and to adorn people. The busy city life gives me inspiration but so does spending time out in the woods."

Casey Newberg — US
/ caseynewberg@gmail.com / caseynewberg.com
Newberg received her MFA from the Tyler School of Art in Philadelphia in 2022, and her undergraduate degree from Kendall College of Art and Design in Grand Rapids, Michigan in 2018. Shortly after leaving undergrad, her family was diagnosed with a rare neurodegenerative disease that is genetic and incurable. Upon receiving this news, she began to focus on the ephemerality and often rotten nature of life. As she continued in graduate school Newberg began developing work that focused on impermanence and followed lines of medical dependence and consumption. Her work focuses on feelings of adulthood displacement and clouded trauma by placing familiar objects in malignant contexts. Many of the pieces she creates incorporate foul language or rotten materials that will self-destruct.

Cassandra Prinzi — AUSTRALIA
/ cassprinzi@hotmail.com
Cassandra is a contemporary jewellery artist working in Melbourne/Naarm. She studied at Melbourne's RMIT University, completing a Bachelor of Arts (Fine Arts) with Honours.
Motivated by play and an affection for colour, she makes jewellery and objects inspired by the natural world. An avid saw-piercer, her material of choice is copper, appreciated for its versatile qualities and humble nature. Teetering between the familiar and the imaginary, her work celebrates colour and the beauty of the world. Cassandra is committed to building a practice that aligns closely with her values around sustainability and the preservation of the environment.

Catalina Rivera — PERU
/ catalinariverajoyas@gmail.com
"I studied architecture in Peru, and my interest in heritage conservation led me to focus my training on monument res-

toration, carrying out specialization studies in Rome, Bologna, and Zaragoza, where I currently live and where I had the opportunity to reinvent myself professionally studying jewellery arts at the School of Art. My training as an architect and my experiences as a student in Europe are reflected in my designs. I have participated in numerous exhibitions with different pieces and with my final degree project, the latter in the Art and Talent space at the Madrid Jewellery Trade Show 2022, where I received the 'Training and knowledge award' for my project 'Tensionadas', inspired by tensile architecture and the work of German architect Frei Otto."

Chao-Hsien Kuo — TAIWAN
/ chao@chaoeero.com / www.chao-hsienkuo.com
Chao-Hsien Kuo is a Finnish contemporary jewellery maker and Master Goldsmith and was awarded Goldsmith of the Year 2022 in Finland. She has been working in the jewellery field since 2004, and actively exhibiting her work around the world. Kuo looks at nature with her heart and finds inspiration in all seasons. Her jewellery interprets simple beauty she sees and experiences in her daily surroundings. She works mainly with precious materials and traditional techniques. Her pieces are very sculptural and her unique form language is highly recognizable in different subjects she works on. Kuo's jewellery is always skilfully made with a delicate touch and shines with effortless elegance.

Chok Shin Ni — SINGAPORE
/ www.shinnjewellery.com
Shin Ni is a contemporary jeweller based in Singapore, and founder of Shinn Jewellery. She studied in Florence at the Alchimia Contemporary Jewellery School in 2017-2018, and works as a full-time artist. With her background in sociology and non-profit work, her artistic practice not only combines her interests in social issues with metallurgy and traditional metalsmithing techniques, but also serves as a medium for meaningful inquiry into the human condition.

Christa Lühtje — GERMANY
/ www.christaluehtje.com
Apprenticeship in Hamburg followed by studies at the Academy of Fine Arts in Munich. Since then, she has been working as a freelance artist. Capturing the beautiful, expressing it in jewellery.

Christoph Straube — GERMANY
/ mail@christoph-straube.de
/ www.christoph-straube.de
"In 1994-1997 I did an apprenticeship as a goldsmith. After some years of practice, I was studying jewellery design at the Akademie der Bildenden Künste in Nuremberg, earning the Meisterschüler title in 2015. In 2008 I had a university teaching position there. From 2009–2013 I was a consultant at the Pakistan Institute of Fashion and Design, Lahore, Pakistan. I have had my own studio in Nuremberg from 2006 and take part in exhibitions and fairs like SCHMUCK at the IHM in Munich, Danner-Preis, Grassimesse in Leipzig, Sofa Chicago in the US, Collect in London, UK etc."

Clara del Papa — VENEZUELA
/ claradelpapa@gmail.com
/ www.claradelpapa.com
Italian-Venezuelan artist raised in a South American cultural and artistic environment enriched by the art of Italy where she currently lives. Architect, landscape architect and airplane pilot, her architectural work merges with her knowledge of goldsmithing and silversmithing techniques perfected in renowned Italian schools. Her work is the inquisitive and intriguing result of reflections and experimental games involving metal, whose hard surface she covers with graceful versatility in organic forms that encircle and embrace the body with a natural and soft appearance, creating a dialogue with the body's anatomy, an alternative and personal reading that reinvents the wearability of jewellery. Her work has received several international awards and has been exhibited at important events, museums, and galleries around the world.

Clara Niubò — SPAIN
/ hola@claraniubo.com
/ www.claraniubo.com
Born in Casserres (Berguedà), 1987. Lives and works in Barcelona. Product Design Degree and Postgraduate in children's illustration at UAB, specifically at the Art Design School of EINA, Barcelona. Higher degree of artistic jewellery at the Massana School in Barcelona. She has done specialized courses in different techniques of painting and jewellery at Massana Permanent, Taller Perill, the Industrial School of Arts and Crafts and the jewellery workshop of Jaime Diaz. She has been part of the collective Joyas Sensacionales, coordinated by Silvia Walz, and Quars d'una collective, with the jewellers Carla Garcia, Sandrà Llusà and Maria Diez. Currently, she is part of the 7 Cats collective. Since 2012 she has participated in various national and international exhibitions such as The Summer Festival, Galería Slavik, Viena; Graduate Show 2013, Marzee Gallery, Holland; Coordenadas, Galerie Noel Guyomarc'h, Montreal; among others.

Claudia Vallejo — COLOMBIA
/ @claudiavallejo.joyera
Anthropologist with a degree from Universidad de Los Andes. Jewellery maker by trade, passion, intuition, skill, and perseverance. Her training in contemporary jewellery at the Massana School in Barcelona adds an artistic stamp to her work. Since 1997 she has been giving form to her feelings, thoughts, and dreams in her studio. Her work, which does not follow trends, is consistent and independent. With an abstract language, clear concepts and indefatigable research of materials and alternative techniques her pieces are innovating and refreshing. A yearly collection that narrates a moment, a context, a history. Her commitment to sustainability (environmental, social, and economic) has been at the centre of what she does for many years.

Constanza Nolé — ARGENTINA
/ cotynole@gmail.com / www.fruto.com.ar
FRUTO is a brand created by industrial designer Constanza Nolé. Its intention is to broaden the meaningful horizon of jewellery and the evocative potential of materials through pieces that suggest aesthetic and symbolic experiences. Her work has appeared in exhibitions at the Museo Municipal de Bellas Artes Juan B. Castagnino, the Córdona International Biennial city of design, the Museo de Arte Popular José Hernández, the Museo de las Mujeres, and the Palm Beach Design Showroom.

Corrado De Meo — ITALY
/ corradodemeo@hotmail.com
/ www.demeogioiellisculture.com
"I turned a passion into a profession. As a self-taught artist through workshops with international artists, I was able to better define my interest in contemporary designer jewellery and direct my professional choices. I began to participate in national and international exhibitions in Europe, China, and the United States, to be published and to win prizes. Two works are present at the Museo degli Argenti in Florence and one in the Cominelli collection in San Felice del Benaco. Regarding my work, I like using recycled material, because it allows me to experiment and discover in its transformation, new symbolic languages to communicate my thought and its form."

Cristina Zani — ITALY

/ info@cristinazani.com / www.cristinazani.com
Following a career in corporate communication, Italian born artist Cristina Zani completed her MFA in Jewellery at Edinburgh College of Art in June 2012. In 2011 she was awarded a bursary that enabled her to study jewellery in Seoul for four months. Her present work is influenced by the urban landscape. She approaches the creation of her jewellery in the same way she would compose a story and, like Marco Polo of *Invisible Cities*, she borrows elements from the city's landscape to visually describe it and subtly suggest it to the viewer. While searching for a personal way to elaborate her vision of the urban landscape, she develops forms that are based on subjective observation but invite the viewer to make new personal associations.

D

Dalila Gomes — PORTUGAL

/ info@dalilagomes.com / www.dalilagomes.com
Balance, versatility, precision, and minimalism are some of the principles underlying the work of Dalila Gomes. Having studied for an undergraduate degree at the University of Oporto's Faculty of Architecture prior to pursuing training in metalsmithing and jewellery design—her childhood passion—at the Contacto Directo School, Dalila uses a varied range of influences in her pieces, often blurring the lines between jewellery, sculpture, and architecture. Her creations are shaped from handling the precious metal itself. Simple gestures such as cutting, folding, subtracting, or twisting enable her to explore themes like movement, geometry, optical illusion, and endless feeling, among others.

Danielle Cadef — USA

/ questions@dcadefdesigns.com
/ www.dcadefdesigns.com
"I am fascinated with the ways in which people adorn themselves. Creating wearable art using a variety of materials lets me connect with people of different cultures.
Some of my first memories are of playing in my grandmother's jewelry box, being fascinated by not just the stones, but the construction and details of the jewelry. I wanted to learn how the jewelry was made. I'm mostly self-taught, supplementing my informal education with books, experimentation, video tutorials and jewelry making related forums. Most of my work is inspired by birds and their colors, or the ocean/beach. I use a variety of materials including stones, found objects, mica, shells, sea glass, driftwood, pottery, mother of pearl, silk thread, and fossils."

Daphne Krinos — UK

/ www.daphnekrinos.com
Daphne established her studio practice after leaving Middlesex University in 1980.
Metal is her language and she loves using oxidised or coated silver, and recycled gold. Colour is important in her practice and she often uses translucent stones in her work.
She is inspired by cities, architecture, and art. She enjoys photographing buildings, construction, and demolition sites. The photographs by Bernd and Hilla Becher, as well as sculptures by Donald Judd, and numerous modernist painters are an inspiration.
Having grown up in Greece she attributes her love of making to her grandfather who was a poet, always surrounded by creative and inspiring people. Spending time with him, made her learn to appreciate materials, colours, and shapes. She was able to put all these early influences into practice after completing her design training.

Denis Music — UKRAINE

/ mnk@denismusic.com.ua / www.denismusic.com.ua
Denis Music is a Ukrainian jeweller. Before working as a jewellery maker, he had more than 15 years' experience in graphic design. Denis has no specialized education as a jeweller. In 2012, he completed a short course at the Jewellery College in Kyiv, Ukraine. In 2013, he began his jewellery practice and creating collections every year. In 2021, he completed an intensive jewellery course at the Alchimia Jewellery School, Florence. Denis believes that a piece of jewellery should be something more than just a pretty jewel. What is important is a statement an owner makes to the world. Denis takes the materials, colours and textures as a palette that helps him to create each jewel's character.

Diana Greenwood — UK

/ diana@dianagreenwood.com
/ dianagreenwood.com
After graduating from the Royal College of Art with a Master's Degree in Goldsmithing and Silversmithing in 1993, Diana set up her studio in London with the aid of a Crafts Council Grant. Diana won the P&O Makower Silver Commission for the Crafts Council in 1995 and in 1996 was named best newcomer at the Chelsea Crafts Fair. She was commissioned to make cutlery for the "Sheffield Millennium Canteen" in 1997. Diana's jewellery combines the clean lines of Danish design with a touch of British charm and humour; a celebration of all things flowery and leafy. Her work is a labour of love; intricately hand-pierced flowers and leaves in sterling silver combined with highlights in 18ct gold and semi-precious stones.

Donna D'Aquino — USA

/ donna@donnadaquino.com
/ donnadaquino.com
"Combining geometric lines and vivid colors, my elegant handcrafted jewelry is the culmination of a lifelong fascination with structural elements and a love of clean, vibrant design. The result is lightweight jewelry that is bold, adventurous, and easy to wear. Whether a distinctive one-of-a-kind necklace, or colorful earrings, all my work is handmade using steel, sterling silver, 18 karat gold, and colorful, durable powder-coated brass in a range of colors, ways, and sizes. Working intuitively, I draw upon a cache of visual memories: bridges, elevated roadways, telephone towers, and city scaffolding. Monumental or minimal, a singular art object, or part of a small product line, each jewelry piece provides the wearer an opportunity to comfortably take up a little more space."

Dorothée Loustalot — SWITZERLAND

/ dorothee.loustalot@gmail.com
/ www.dorothee-loustalot.com
Dorothee Loustalot is a jewellery and product designer. Born 27 February 1984 in France, she lives and works in Geneva.
"After a scientific baccalaureate, I first studied Product Design in Lyon, in France. Then, I followed with a Bachelor's in Jewellery and Accessory Design at HEAD-Geneva. In 2009, my degree collection, which combined industrial and traditional craftsmanship, laid the foundation for my personal work. Over the years, I created—always with a kind of ingenious poetry—products and jewels, combining 3D impression and crafty techniques, in collaboration with innovative Swiss firms, which has allowed me to take part in international design and jewellery fairs around the world. Since 2009, I have also been working as a freelancer and a design teacher."

Dot Melanin — ISRAEL

/ dotmelanin@gmail.com
"As a maker, I have never clung to any material or technique. I allow myself to be free. To use any material or technique that will allow my imagination to come to reality. As an assemblage of elements and colours that builds an associative world."

E

Edna Madera — USA
/ emt@ednamadera.com / ednamadera.com
Studio artist, teacher: Pratt Fine Arts Center (Seattle), Penland School of Craft (North Carolina), Arrowmont School of Crafts (Tennessee); education: MFA - Rochester Institute of Technology, BFA - Southern Illinois University. Edna Madera is an American studio jeweller working in Kansas City, Missouri. Edna honed her craft by maintaining a studio practice while working as a bench jeweller and studio assistant. Her technical experience opened opportunities in the jewellery industry. Hired as a product development manager and jewellery designer, Edna learned the ins and outs of global sourcing, product development, and the supply chain. In 2014 Edna opened her namesake studio where her mission is to meld design with technique in fine jewellery.

Edna Milevsky — CANADA
/ edna.milevsky@gmail.com
/ www.ednamilevsky.com
Edna Milevsky is a fellow of the Canadian Gemmological Association and a graduate of George Brown College's Jewellery Arts & Gemmology programmes. In 2019 she was the first runner-up winner at the DeBeers Shining Light Design initiative in Gaborone, Botswana. Edna is currently a goldsmith at Jewel Envy in Toronto, Canada.
Edna is inspired by patterns and textures found in nature. She employs traditional goldsmithing techniques to create perfectly imperfect handmade marks. Equally important is the kinetic quality found in her jewellery. Pearls are featured prominently in many of her pieces.

Edwin Charmain — INDONESIA
/ hello@pusaka.co.uk / www.pusaka.co.uk
Descending from a family of textile producers in the city of Batik, Pekongan, Indonesian-born jewellery designer-maker Edwin Charmain focuses on creating ethical filigree jewellery that is inspired by his country's batik and traditions. By combining traditional Indonesia Batik motifs with unique sequences found in natural objects and buildings, Charmain's work transformed what was once a two-dimensional waing technique on top of fabric into a three-dimensional weaving object. Charmain holds a Master's in Design Jewellery from Central Saint Martins and is one of the Arts Council England's exceptional promise endorsees. His work has been exhibited internationally, and in early 2022 he was selected as the Silver winner for the ready-to-wear category at the UK Goldsmiths' Crafts and Design Council Awards.

Eero Hintsanen — FINLAND
/ eero@chaoeero.com / www.eerohintsanen.com
Both a Master Goldsmith and Master of Arts, Eero Hintsanen traverses the worlds of sculpture and jewellery design. As a designer and artist, he works not only on ranges of wearable jewellery, but also on unique and large pieces whose atmospheres are filled to the brim with old-world mystique. Hintsanen's works carry his signature style, which is bold and with a tough Finnish dimension. His unapologetic approach to reinterpreting the traditional field has earned him the prestigious Goldsmith of the Year 2019 title in Finland.

Elgin Fischer — GERMANY
/ elgin@elginschmuck.de / www.elginschmuck.de
"After a classical goldsmith apprenticeship, I studied jewellery design at the University of Applied Sciences in Düsseldorf, graduating in 2002. Thanks to a scholarship, I was then able to learn many "old" techniques, including enamelling.
This knowledge of techniques and design led to the development of the EMAILLESCHMUCK collection, which I exhibit at trade fairs and now sell at many galleries in Germany and abroad. There are two main reasons why I have focused more and more on this technique: one is the idiosyncrasy of the material and the accuracy of the technique. In addition, enamelling allows for a very special design line: by reducing to basic geometric shapes, the focus can be directed to one of my favourite materials: coloured glass."

Elif Ustunel — TURKEY
/ elif@elifustunel.com
"I'm an Istanbul-based jeweller. I design and make by hand all the jewellery in my studio in the heart of Istanbul. My metalsmithing journey started in the Grand Bazaar. I learnt traditional goldsmith techniques and materials from the masters. I worked in Senay Akin's atelier as her assistant before I opened my own studio. Throughout my career I have had the opportunity to transform all this knowledge into a contemporary style. And I'm mostly inspired by Prehistoric and Ancient Art."

Ellen Cohen — USA
/ ellen@ellencohendesign.com
/ https://ellencohendesign.com
"Like life, my work is unpredictable. Grit, natural beauty and the unexpected all play a part. Form and texture are embodied in my work. Primitive and bold, ancient, and modern, I strive to bring beauty out of chaos. Amulets and shields appear in my work. These are a reaction to my need to protect myself and those I care about from the blatant disregard for the Earth, radical politics, and social tension.
My jewelry is meant to stand the test of time, honoring the earth and the individuals who wear it. Trained in ornamental horticulture and graphic design, my bench is where all worlds meet."

Els Vansteelandt — BELGIUM
/ els.vansteelandt@skynet.be
/ www.elsvansteelandt.be
Els Vansteelandt started as an independent gold and silversmith in 1997. She designs jewellery and objects. Her work is displayed in galleries in major cities in Europe. Since 2010, she has run her own creative lab and gallery in Brussels. Design Flanders took her work to the World Best Design Exchange in Seoul. She has also been selected twice for the German Silver Triennial. "The emotional impulses I get from the environment lead me to precious metal, and from then on, it's the material that takes the lead. So, my creations can spontaneously occur at any moment while working. The physical properties play an important role in my creative process. Their boundaries and obstacles provide new challenges and ideas."

Elvira Cibotti — ARGENTINA
/ elviracibotti@gmail.com / www.elviracibotti.com.ar
"I started making jewellery in 2007. I have trained over the years in different courses and workshops that have allowed me to find my own way of expression and speak through my work on issues that are meaningful to me.
When I started looking for a material to add to my work, to make my process more personal, my first choice was paper. I wanted to recycle it but also to reuse all those images and publications that would be discarded. Give them a second chance, a second life. The result grabbed me in such a way that it became my raw material. Since then, it's a one-way trip full of experimentations and discoveries."

Emily Culver — USA
/ emilyculverstudio@gmail.com
/ www.emily-culver.com
Emily Culver is a multimedia object maker and educator originally from rural Pennsylvania. She received her Bachelor of Fine Arts in Metals/Jewelry/CAD-CAM from the Tyler School of Art and Architecture in 2012. In 2017 she received her Master

of Fine Arts in Metalsmithing from Cranbrook Academy of Art. In addition to exhibiting her work internationally Culver also teaches at craft schools and universities across America. Existing primarily as sculpture, objects and jewellery, Culver's work explores notions of intimacy, (non)functionality, gender, and identity through corporeal qualities.

Erica Bello — USA

/ ericabellojewelry@gmail.com
/ ericabellojewelry.com

Since 2013, Erica Bello has created multi-dimensional work that bridges the gap between traditional and contemporary jewellery. With an interest in the reinterpretation of classic iconography, she looks to recurring motifs in art and culture for inspiration. Classically trained, Erica explores traditional metalsmithing techniques alongside digital design. The result is in her own immediately recognizable work that falls somewhere between classic and contemporary. Erica Bello studied metals/jewellery design at the School for American Crafts where she earned her BFA. Erica's work has been showcased at New York Jewelry Week, The Museum of Art and Design, SOFA Chicago, and can be found internationally in several contemporary craft galleries. Erica currently resides in Providence, RI.

Esperança Leria — BRAZIL

/ eleria@uol.com.br
/ www.esperancaleria.com.br

With a degree in architecture and urbanism, she started to dedicate herself exclusively to author jewellery in 2018. She sees projects as a natural way of organizing thoughts and as a support in the making of jewellery, but she discovered experimentation of materials and manual work as an important part of her creative process and form of expression.
Movement, transparency, and overlays are present in the composition, textures and colours of her pieces and express the daily life, the feminine and nature.
"What touches me is what inspires me."

Esteban Erosky — MEXICO

/ estebanerosky@gmail.com

"Jewellery and fire enamelling are the artistic language of my work, which takes place on the border between the fun and the violent, the strange and the childish, death and laughter, between candy and viscera, vindicating the human species by exposing its weaknesses and virtues. These creations have been selected and awarded in several international contests and exhibited in galleries and museums in different countries such as Spain, Israel, Switzerland, the United States, Portugal, and China."

Ester Ferret Totosaus — SPAIN

/ esterft@gmail.com / www.esterferret.com

"After studying interior design and industrial design and working for several years in the sector, I thought it would be better to design and make my own objects. I studied different disciplines in the jewellery sector such as fired enamel, engraving, setting, forging, pearl stranding and Berber jewellery. I studied at the Escuela Industrial in Barcelona, the Massana School, and the Barcelona Jeweller's Association. Jewellery gave me the opportunity to create my pieces and study to forge a path in this new medium. Currently, I work in jewellery, trends, and fashion, broadening my technical and artistic horizons."

Eszter Sára Kocsor — HUNGARY

/ kocsor.eszter.sara@gmail.com
/ www.esztersarakocsor.com

A jewellery designer based in Budapest, Eszter Sára Kocsor seeks to give her wearers a glimpse of a different world. Her "Mirror in Mirror" collection came to life during the time she spent in Hildesheim, Germany. Her black and gold PVD coated stainless steel jewellery is made with a point welding laser, put together piece by piece with utmost precision. Some of her pieces feature zirconia stones and various gems in their centre. "I wanted to define myself as precisely as possible. I have always been a bit insecure, however, while creating, I have always felt a deep knowledge and determination of what I want to do. My jewellery is a symbol of that determination and dedication I always wanted to feel inside me."

Eugènia Arnavat Rosselló — SPAIN

"I have a degree in fine arts and am a jeweller, gemmologist, and diamond specialist. Since 1995 I have taught jewellery at EAD Tarragona, where I was department coordinator. I have received jewellery awards and have had and curated solo and group exhibitions. Jewellery is an artistic and communication medium that allows me to ask questions, present a world view – it is a space of self-knowledge and tool for social commitment. My pieces are the fruit of concepts, sensations, thoughts; they seek beauty and simplicity."

F

Fernando Haro — SPAIN

/ fdo_haro.rguez@hotmail.com

"I began my jewellery studies in Seville, focusing on fired enamel techniques. Today, I work in Valencia, more focused on design and artistic jewellery. I am always searching for new techniques, materials, and inspiration to nurture my creativity. Devoting myself to jewellery is something personal through which I express my concerns, feelings, and ideas. I base my work mainly on a concept and then I let my imagination run wild. I try to interact with the observer and facilitate an exchange of thoughts."

Florian Wagner — GERMANY

/ info@floschmuck.at / www.floschmuck.at

The unique use of precious metals and stones, in addition to first-class workmanship, is of prime importance for Florian Wagner's jewellery. But we never lose sight of the ultimate goal, namely: the wearability of a piece of jewellery, in tune with the person who is wearing it. The artist feels compelled to highlight both the inner and exterior images of the client. Florian Wagner's strongest source of inspiration is music. "Art nouveau paintings and an awareness of the beguiling qualities of the materials themselves inspired my creation of this pair of earrings, dedicated to the female desire for self-adornment."

G

Gabriela Sierra Torres — MEXICO

/ gabyst87@me.com / @gabrielasierramx

"I have a degree in Industrial Design from ITESM Oro. My first contact with jewellery making was at the Alchimia School in Florence in 2014, where I learned basic jewellery techniques from amazing masters. Upon returning to Mexico, I worked for six years in the packaging industry until in 2021, I came out with my own jewellery brand. While I am a newcomer to the world of jewellery, I was selected for Milan Jewellery Week 2022 and I will also participate in Cluster Jewellery in London next December. With my brand I seek to promote the revaluation of the goldsmithing craft and reflect the slow-made process through unique sculptural pieces."

Gabriele Hinze — GERMANY

/ hinze.gabriele@outlook.de / www.gabrielehinze.de

Born in 1964 in Essen, Gabriele Hinze completed her goldsmith's apprenticeship and worked as a goldsmith until 1990. After her studies at t Düsseldorf University of Applied Sciences, in 1995 she co-founded the Jewellery Gallery SchmuckProdukt in Essen. From 2005 until 2008 she was a temporary lecturer at Düsseldorf University of Applied Sciences. Since 2008 Gabriele Hinze has worked as a freelance jewellery artist in Berlin, where she recently established her workspace at SCHMUCKE Gallery. "Making jewellery is to me: getting involved in a dialogue. A dialogue between imagination and doing, craftsmanship and material, act and effect, effort and giving or resisting, patience and perseverance, planning, and coincidence, being made and having become."

Gayane Avetisyan — ARMENIA
/ gayane8@yahoo.com
/ www.gayaneavetisyan.ca

Armenian-born Gayane Avetisyan is a multidisciplinary artist who received her formative art education in printmaking, pottery and oil painting. Ten years ago, she discovered her passion for metalsmithing and enamelling, a medium she now uses to express her perspectives on contemporary life. Since then, she combines traditional and alternative enamelling techniques to create her one-of-a-kind art jewellery. She has participated in exhibitions and competitions in her adopted city of Montreal, Canada as well as internationally. Most recently, she received an award for excellence in technique at the prestigious Romanian Jewellery Week.

Gésine Hackenberg — GERMANY
/ mail@gesinehackenberg.com
/ www.gesinehackenberg.com

Gésine Hackenberg uses diverse techniques to explore the conceptual overlap between jewellery and objects of everyday life. She looks at how domestic objects and materials relate to the individual and the body. Gésine was trained as a goldsmith in Germany and graduated in 2001 from the Gerrit Rietveld Academie in Amsterdam (NL). In 2013 she earned her MA from the PXL-MAD School of Arts in Hasselt (BE) where she also taught. Hackenberg received several grants and awards. Her work is included in various public collections such as the Stedelijk Museum Amsterdam (NL), the Victoria and Albert Museum in London (UK) and the MAD in NY (USA). The earrings from the Ceramic Jewellery Collection celebrate decorative collectibles in ceramics and the emotional value they bear for many people.

Giulia Savino — ITALY
/ info@giuliasavino.com
/ www.giuliasavino.com

Giulia Savino is an Italian contemporary jewellery designer with an international background. After receiving a bachelor's degree in Fashion Design, she obtained a Masters in Contemporary Jewellery from the Alchimia School in Florence. She is successfully managing her career combining studio practice with teaching. Since 2018 she has been the head of the jewellery department at Istituto Europeo di Design (IED) in Milan; she is also a design teacher. She is currently living in Turin where, in 2018, she opened her studio. Her research is defined by a visual approach. Everyday experiences are represented by images, elaborated into precious jewels. They respond to very contemporary needs: they are seducing and light objects, take up little space and adapt to different contexts.

H

Heather Guidero — USA
/ studio@heatherguidero.com
/ www.heatherguidero.com

Heather Guidero received a BFA in Jewellery and Metalsmithing from the Rhode Island School of Design in 2002. Following a three-year apprenticeship as a goldsmith in NYC, Heather returned to Rhode Island to teach and develop her own collections. Seventeen years later, Heather Guidero Jewelry is an established studio that designs and produces modernist inspired fine and functional jewellery handmade in Providence, Rhode Island, using recycled gold and silver accented with ethically sourced gem stones. The collections are carried in stores and galleries across the USA.

Heejoo Kim — REPUBLIC OF KOREA
/ heejoo.km@gmail.com / heejookim.com

"I began my study of the craft at Kookmin University in Seoul. In 2008 I went to Pforzheim University in Germany as an exchange student, and it was the starting point of my intensive research into jewellery and electroforming technique. From my first solo show 'Fifth Season' in 2011, research continued with jewellery focused on the reinterpretation of traditional techniques, leading to my second individual show "<UniverShell>" in 2020. My works are archived in permanent public collections, including the Seoul Craft Museum and the Museum of Decorative Arts in Paris. Currently, I am focusing on presenting novel images of Korean traditional crafts and history based on my research."

Heidemarie Herb — GERMANY

Heidemarie Herb trained as a goldsmith in Kempten, and was certified in 1991, in Munich, Germany. She attended various courses, conferences, and workshops.

Her works have been displayed in books, catalogues, and several prominent exhibitions in more than 15 countries around the world. She has been honoured with different awards in Poland, Russia, and Italy. Her works are in the permanent collections in the Amber Museum (PL), Malbork Castle Museum (PL), and the Cominelli Foundation (IT), as well as in private collections in Austria, USA, and Lithuania. "In my work, the interplay of colour and form, accuracy and imperfection are fundamental to create a harmonious overall picture. I prefer to combine pigments with silver or use old materials such as rusted iron, objects I found or old forgotten parts of these last. Working them out and giving them a new feeling of being is what I most like to do."

Helena Aguilar — COLOMBIA
/ helenaaguilarespaciodejoyeria@gmail.com
/ www.helenaaguilar.com

Helena Aguilar is an industrial designer by training, an award-winning jewellery maker with over 30 years of experience, and a teacher by profession. In the search for a career that allowed her to create and express herself, she found jewellery. Since then, it has been her focus of reflection and means of promoting her brand Helenaguilar. It also allows her to share and transmit her methodology, which she has been perfecting for years, through her workshop, which she named Jewellery Space, to help the people who happen upon it find their personal language.

Helena Romanova — UKRAINE
/ www.helenaromanova.com

The brand HELENA ROMANOVA is a jewellery and accessories business, established by fashion designer Olena Romanova, who has been creating her masterpieces since 2010, in Kyiv, Ukraine. Olena Romanova has been a resident of Ukrainian Fashion Week since 2015, presenting its own collections and creating accessories for catwalk shows of other designers. "Our creations are widely used in looks for magazine photoshoots (Vogue, Harper's Bazaar, etc.) events, and video recordings by Ukrainian and European celebrities and musicians."

Heng Lee — TAIWAN
/ henglee1017@msn.com / @henglee1017

Heng Lee graduated from the Graduate Institute of Applied Arts at TNNUA in 2011. In 2012, he established the creative brand of contemporary jewellery Heng Lee Jewellery and achieved great success in international exhibitions and competitions, including winning the New Traditional Jewellery Design Contest in Netherlands, and the BKV-Prize 2013 for Young Applied Arts in Bavaria, Germany, as well as being selected for the Fifth International Biennial of Enamel Art in Lithuania. In 2015, he became part of the initiative to retain local talent by the Kaohsiung Bureau of Cultural Affairs and established the first contemporary jewellery art space in Kaohsiung, "PIN sstudio". In the past few years, he has invited many jewellery artists from home and abroad to Kaohsiung for exhibitions and lectures and has curated international jewellery exhibitions, facilitating Taiwan's communication with the world.

Ignasi Cavaller Triay — SPAIN
/ ignasicavaller@gmail.com / www.ignasicavaller.com
He began with jewellery when he was sixteen in Menorca, continuing his studies at the Massana School (Barcelona) and Karelia University of Applied Sciences (Lappeenranta), and completing them at Trier University of Applied Sciences (Idar-Oberstein). He has taught in Cairo and Barcelona. Recently he returned to Menorca where he is developing new projects that will soon be completed. His work has been exhibited in galleries and museums around the world, and he has received various international awards over the course of his career. His jewellery also appears in several books.

Inesa Kovalova — UKRAINE
/ inesa.kovalova@gmail.com / www.inesakovalova.com
Inesa's professional path is characterized by the change of scales and cultures. Born in Ukraine, her design career started in architecture, after which she studied art and design in Italy and the renowned Central Saint Martins in London. Influenced by the exploration of relationships between material, craftsmanship and design embraced by early twentieth century French modernist jewellers, Inesa Kovalova aspires to reinvent our understanding of luxury jewellery in the context of shifting values and the urgency of sustainability. Art, design, and architecture-inspired, Inesa's pieces range from re-defined precious classics to contemporary 3D printed art jewels.

Iris Nijenhuis — THE NETHERLANDS
/ info@irisnijenhuis.com / www.irisnijenhuis.com
Iris Nijenhuis is an Amsterdam-based designer with a passion for laser cutting and a wide interest in experimental shapes and structures. In 2011 she graduated from the Amsterdam Fashion Institute with a collection of fabrics and unique pieces that emerged from broad research into the use of innovative techniques. She tried to extend the value of textile by extracting the essence and adding functionality to the fabric. By experimenting with laser cutting, she developed a technique in which the fabric is cut into small puzzle pieces that form the basis of the design process. By connecting the puzzle pieces together manually, inspiring shapes and structures are created that can form various products.

Iris Saar – inSync design — AUSTRALIA
/ iris@insyncdesign.com.au
/ https://insyncdesign.com.au
"My work is an evolving process where graphic design meets contemporary jewellery. I strive to create distinct and whimsical wearable art that is practical and comfortable to wear. For the past 15 years, I have been running the award-winning studio inSync design that aims to create high-quality Australian made, contemporary jewellery that is unique, timeless, and affordable. inSync maintains a fiercely independent approach to contemporary jewellery, whilst marrying cutting-edge technology with traditional practices to craft clever jewellery of exceptional quality that is available in more than seventy prestigious galleries and museum stores internationally."

Isabelle Hertzeisen — SWITZERLAND
/ isabelle.hertzeisen@gmail.com
/ www.isabellehertzeisen.ch
Isabelle Hertzeisen is a jewellery designer who works and lives in Lucerne, Switzerland. Her pieces are the fruit of the meeting of her technical training as a watchmaker with her main sources of inspiration: nature and everyday observations.

Jacqueline Morren — THE NETHERLANDS
/ jacky.morren@gmail.com
"The body of work 'Golden' is made using refurbished gold and silver, combined with NZ Pounamu/Jade. Mindful of dwindling resources, together with the high ecological cost of mining, I consciously challenge myself to minimize my use of materials in creating these durable pieces without sacrificing the designs. I was introduced to New Zealand's precious stone, jade, in 2000 and from that moment on I was captivated by the green stone. All components are made and formed by hand using raw materials. My work is represented in various galleries throughout New Zealand."

Jan Smith — CANADA
/ jansmithca@hotmail.com / www.jansmith.ca
Jan Smith is an artist working with vitreous enamel in combination with altered and textured metals. Jan's jewellery and metalwork employ traditional enamelling in combination with contemporary techniques; allowing for the exploration of imagery and mark making. Smith's work has a tactile delicacy and the marks create a language or code; this is an invented language, a code that affords her a dialogue with the natural world. Born in Vancouver BC, Smith holds Canadian & American citizenship. Jan received her BFA from Nova Scotia College of Art & Design in Halifax, NS. She studied metalsmithing and enamelling in the US.

Jeffrey Lloyd Dever — USA
/ jeff@deverdesigns.com / jeffreylloyddever.com
Trained in graphic design, Jeffrey Lloyd Dever has worked and taught design, illustration, and jewellery techniques for over 25 years. His work is held in numerous museums and private collections. He considers all his jewellery miniature sculptural studies. The fact that they are wearable at all is almost incidental to the aesthetics he seeks. Each is born through sketches which mature into fabricated forms of polymer clay, either built over reinforced armatures or form built hollow forms. Through repeated cycles of fabrication, veneering and oven curing, his pieces grow slowly layer by layer. Each colour gradient and surface details are the actual colour of the clay. A single piece can easily go through 15-20 fabrication/curing cycles, and take weeks to complete.

Jennie Gill — UK
/ info@jenniegill.co.uk / www.jenniegill.co.uk
Jennie has been creating from studios in Sheffield since 1991. Initially designing for the high street and brands, she now works on single pieces and commissions.
Her work has a raw energy and takes reference from the industrial heritage of her surroundings. She is known for her honest use of materials, often leaving flaws and natural edges exposed, celebrating the natural and organic materials she works with. A modern take on handmade tradition, Jennie's work is held in many private collections worldwide.

Jenny Llewellyn — UK
/ www.jennyllewellyn.com
Jenny Llewellyn is an award winning, contemporary jewellery designer-maker based at Cockpit Arts, London. She graduated from Middlesex University in 2007 with a BA (Hons) in Jewellery. Inspired by the luminous colours, shapes and movement of underwater life, Jenny's work is characterised by handcrafted, organic forms of precious metals combined with vibrant bursts of silicone. Jenny's practice is driven by experimentation. She experiments with colour and with material, combining precious with non-precious, to create tactile and fun pieces, available in the full spectrum of colours, from discreet pops of monochrome, to full statement colour-fades. Central to Jenny's practice is her pioneering use of silicone. Often mistaken for

Kristina started in jewellery art at only one-year old, when she drew her first ring in her father's workshop. All in all, she has spent 40 years in the world of jewellery, the last 20 as a professional artist and designer. She acquired her Master of Fine Arts and Jewellery Design at Kiev National University of Construction and Architecture. Driven by family values and a passion to create, the brand LIÉNA jewels combines the legacy of classical jewellery art and innovation in one-of-a-kind pieces and bespoke jewellery for private customers and collectors.

Laura Sophia Herrlich — GERMANY
/ laura.herrlich@t-online.de

Laura Herrlich is a state-approved designer of jewellery and objects who attended the technical college for design, jewellery and objects at the Goldsmith and Watchmaking Academy Pforzheim (Germany). Currently she studies jewellery and tableware at this school. The featured earrings were inspired by insects, more specifically beetles. The earrings were implemented with the CAD program and then cast in 925/- silver.
The earrings have two sides. Outside the pieces are oxidised and white. And inside they are coloured in blue and green. However, these colours are not recognisable at first sight.

Lavinia Rossetti — ITALY
/ rossetti.lvn@gmail.com
/ www.laviniarossetti.com

Lavinia Rossetti is an Italian jewellery maker based in Florence. She investigates the performative possibilities of jewellery by creating pieces that generate a bond with the movements of the wearer. Her works assume multiple shapes when in contact with the body. Rossetti taught at Alchimia Contemporary Jewellery School in Florence from 2014 -2018. She then moved to Shanghai where she collaborated and led workshops at the Academy of International Visual Arts, Shanghai Institute of Visual Art, and SanW Gallery/Studio. Rossetti currently travels to Milan where she teaches at IED (European Institute of Design) and works out of her studio in the heart of Florence. She is represented by Antonella Villanova Gallery and her works are shown internationally in exhibitions and design fairs.

Lena Wunderlich — GERMANY
/ contact@lenawunderlich.de
/ www.lenawunderlich.de

Approaching jewellery from outside of the binary, Lena Wunderlich's work seeks to break the traditions of gendered design. Playing with simplicity, her series of work uses shape and weight to create balance in a world obsessed with duality. Using contrasting materials like silicone and metal, Wunderlich looks to find equilibriums where the negative spaces are just as important as the positive. Based in Germany, Lena initially trained as a goldsmith through the Chamber of Handicraft of East Westphalia before going on to receive a BA in Integrated Design at Cologne International School of Design and a Master of Fine Arts in Jewellery and Metalsmithing from the Rhode Island School of Design.

Leticia Llera Martínez — MEXICO
/ info@leticiallera.com / www.leticiallera.com

Leticia Llera grew up with the paradigm of being different from everybody. It didn't matter how. That's why she always kept herself busy with activities that helped her imagination grow. She comes from a creative family, which led her to an amazing career in design. She studied Technical Jewellery Goldsmithing in the National Institute of the Fine Arts, where she found in metals the perfect way to express herself and add her DNA to unconventional pieces. Leticia Llera Joya has been working for more than 32 years to promote the unique design of jewellery created in Mexico. For this designer, it's a great satisfaction to develop a concept and tell a story in every piece or collection that's done in her workshop, which contributes to preserving and carrying on a bit of Mexican beauty.

Liaung Chung Yen — TAIWAN
/ liaung@yahoo.com
/ www.liaungchungyen.com

Liaung Chung Yen was born and raised in Taiwan and his jewellery and artistic aesthetic is influenced by Chinese culture and art. Yen sees his work as an expression of the mind as well as small sculptures documenting the time and emotions in which he lives. Yen received his Master of Fine Arts in Metals and Jewellery from the Savannah College of Art and Design (SCAD). Prior to this he studied Industrial Art at the National Taiwan University of Art in Taiwan. Liaung Chung Yen is the recipient of numerous awards including MJSA Vision Awards, New York Foundation for the Arts Fellowship, and the NICHE Award. He appears in numerous publications. His work has been selected in several prestigious shows such as the Philadelphia Museum of Art Contemporary Craft Show, Smithsonian Craft Show, and Sculpture Objects Functional Art + Design (SOFA), Chicago.

Liisa Hashimoto — JAPAN
/ hinge@sage.ocn.ne.jp / www.hinge-dept.com

"I make contemporary jewellery and objects in Osaka, Japan. I always get inspired by walking outside, looking around parks, buildings, and houses, and so on. The little movement and balances of the parks reflect their character in my jewellery work and objects, too. I am also attracted by little seeds, buds, fresh leaves coming out and mosses growing around the waterside. The organic variety of nature, such as different shapes and forms, seasonal changes, is so fascinating. For my jewellery I hope that people feel happy and smile wearing them."

Lisa Black — USA
/ info@lisablackjewellery.com
/ www.lisablackjewellery.com

Jewellery designer Lisa Black is a native New Yorker, currently living in the coastal region of Australia. A keen observer of the natural world and collector of ancient ornaments, Lisa interlaces found treasures and gemstones into bespoke items of adornment. Her background in landscape architecture underpins attention to detail and unusual combinations of texture and colour, enabling the actualization of her passions.
An enthusiastic believer in the process, the pursuit of reviving time-worn relics reinvented into cherished items of beauty.

Lluís Comín — SPAIN
/ info@lluiscomin.com
/ www.comin-joieriacreativa.com

"I was born in Barcelona in 1958. I learned the trade from my father, but I also attended the Massana School where I began to give shape to concepts which I had only intuited. I am also a gemmologist, a title received from the University of Barcelona. Jewellery is not only adornment. It is my means of artistic expression. The mountains, for me, are almost a religion. It's like an "umbilical cord" that connects me to a world that I deeply love. I have a shop/studio in Barcelona. I participate in international exhibitions, and my pieces are in several private collections in the United States and Europe, as well as in some museums. Currently, I am a member of the governing body of the JORGC, from which I received the artisan's award in 2017. "

Lucy Martin — UK
/ www.lucymartin.co.uk

Contemporary fine jewellery exploring a fascination with colour and contrast. "My work is characterised by graphic forms in which precisely balanced sequences of colour and texture are suspended. Gemstones are carefully selected and often individually cut for my designs. Despite using simple tools and ancient techniques I like to create a very sleek look by concealing connections and fixings wherever possible, keeping the focus on the gemstones and their unique natural qualities. Each piece is handcrafted in recycled metals." Lucy lives and works in London, where she grew up, establishing her own workshop in 2002. She completed her initial jewellery training at Birmingham School of Jewellery and later gained an MA from Central Saint Martins.

Lucy Spink — UK
/ lucy@lucyspinkjewellery.co.uk
/ lucyspinkjewellery.co.uk
"My aim is to create jewellery which is easy for everyone to wear yet thought provoking in the message it carries. As someone who walks in the countryside and sees the changes in the seasons at close quarters, I want to remind people that our natural environment is precious. Now more so than ever, we need to think carefully about our place in the world."

Mar Sánchez — SPAIN
/ marsanchezjoyas@gmail.com
/ www.marsanchezjoyas.com
She studied at the Higher School of Design (Balearic Islands), the Massana School, Escola d'Art del Treball, Taller Perill (Barcelona) and the Tarragona School of Art and Design, in addition to participating in numerous workshops and obtaining a Masters in Contemporary Jewellery Braincelona (Barcelona). Her work has been recognized with several awards and mentions and exhibited in different European countries, in addition to being present in various Spanish cities. She sees jewellery as an art form more than an ornament. Her work is based on experimentation and her pieces are the result of searching and a look inward.

Maren Düsel — GERMANY
/ info@marenduesel.com / www.marenduesel.com
Maren Düsel is a jewellery designer and jewellery artist from Düsseldorf. She studied Applied Art and Design in Düsseldorf. In 2013 she founded her own studio, Atelier Hinter Indien. Her work is characterised by a minimalist formal language and striking colour accents. By making use of unusual materials, she develops a distinctive aesthetic. The artist uses well-known goldsmith techniques, as well as modern approaches such as 3D-printing techniques. The result is graphic jewellery pieces which stand out with timeless design. Maren Düsel's work can be found in numerous exhibitions and in national and international galleries.

Margo Nelissen — THE NETHERLANDS
/ margonelissen@planet.nl
/ www.margonelissen.nl
Margo Nelissen is a jewellery designer who designs unique pieces and small collections inspired by different themes. Steadily and organically, she's expanding her oeuvre like growing branches on a tree. The collection "Hidden" is about how we interact and how we show or hide our motivations, secrets, and scars. We wear masks to protect ourselves and not feel vulnerable. If we open our hearts, we feel exposed. But it also makes us feel strong. We shine and attract attention. These pieces have a clear inside and outside. The outside is like a protective shield that doesn't give away easily its treasured inside. The wearer chooses how to wear the pieces and thus communicates their mood with the world.

Maria Avillez — PORTUGAL
/ maria.avillez.almeida@gmail.com
/ maria.avillez.jewellery.com
After several years in the field of graphic design, Maria found in jewellery a more manual and artistic path and decided to take a course at the Contacto Directo school in Lisbon. She also took the Silverware course at ARCO and the 3D Rhinoceros course, Japanese lacquer, and cutting and setting at Contacto Directo. The artist exhibited in a few schools and international jewellery fairs such as BIJOHCA in France, INORGENTA in Germany, and also at the Portojoia fair in Portugal. She now has her own atelier in Lisbon. Her work is characterised by graphic and simple forms, exploring different materials. Maria designs by instinct and is inspired by nature and urban forms.

Maria Rosa Franzin — ITALY
/ mariarosafranzin11@gmail.com
From 1986 to 2018 she has taught goldsmith design at Pietro Selvatico in Padua. In the last three years she has held Goldsmith design courses at Beijing Institute Fashion Technology China. She lives and works in Padua. Since 2013 she has been the chairperson of AGC Association Contemporary Jewellery.

Marina Sheetikoff — BRAZIL
/ marinasheetikoff@gmail.com
/ www.marinasheetikoff.com
"In contemporary jewellery, I found not only a cultural sign of communication between people, but also a medium to express with freedom. My work encompasses feelings, memories, stories, and I'm fuelled by nature with the impact of human presence reflecting in our ecosystem. Working in my own studio since 2000, with individual exhibitions in 2017 and 2018 at Alice Floriano Gallery, in 2013 I conceived and curated the exhibition 'Projeto Corrente' at the ACASA Museu do Objeto Brasileiro. International selected group exhibitions: 'Tanto Mar', MUDE, Portugal; 'Vecinos', Museum of Popular Art José Hernandez, Buenos Aires, Argentina; Contemporary Jewelry in Íbero-America, SNBA , Lisbon, Portugal; 'Metallophone – Bonds', Gallery AV17, Vilnius, Lithuania; Grupo Broca, 1:11-SNBA, Lisbon, Portugal; 2015 Beijing International Biennial of Contemporary Jewelry, China, among others."

Mark Nuell — UK
/ info@marknuell.com
/ www.marknuell.com
Mark Nuell is a goldsmith and lapidary artist. His fascination with jewellery and gemstones came at an early age in Rubyvale, Australia,where his father was a sapphire miner for nearly 30 years. This inspired Mark to study lapidary and jewellery making in Sydney. Currently Mark is based in London. However, he still visits the local miners in Australia, maintaining a close relationship and giving him unique access to rare and beautiful sapphires. Mark is a master of the lapidary art, which has become a dying craft. He uses his experience and knowledge to accentuate the gemstones' natural beauty, faceting the gems into unique freeform designs from his London studio. With 30 years of goldsmithing experience, Mark integrates the gems into exquisite jewellery pieces.

Marta Alonso — SPAIN
/ hola@martaalonsojewels.com
/ www.martaalonsojewels.com
"I am an interior designer and since 2014, I have taken jewellery courses in different workshops and schools such as Taller Perill, Taller de Jaime Diaz, Alchimia, and finally in 2019, I started a degree in jewellery at the Massana School. I became interested in jewellery through my need for creative freedom, going back to working with my hands on a small scale and escaping from so much screen time. In this art, I enjoy creating, without limits, artistic and author jewellery. My curious mind, my inquisitiveness about artisan work, my love of art and arts & crafts, of travel and learning about new cultures, and my sensibility, connect me to the need to create."

Marta Coderque — SPAIN

/ coderque@coderque.com
/ www.coderque.com

After training as a gemmologist, designer, and jeweller, her first choice was to follow her passion: gemmology, an activity that she combines with designing commissioned pieces. The need to mine that vein of creativity pushed her to design several collections in the purest artisanal tradition, which she now also combines with more recent technologies. Following the enthusiastic reception of her unique pieces, she founded the company Coderque Jewels. Her collections are replete with silver and gold, combining precious metals with natural stones. Her work can be divided into fun & original everyday-wear pieces with a limited production and commissioned & unique pieces for customers looking for a special creation.

Marta Ortí — SPAIN

/ info@martaorti.com / www.martaorti.com

Marta Ortí is a graphic designer and jewellery maker who lives and works in Terrassa, Catalonia. In 2005 she entered the world of design, specialising in Graphic Design at the School of Art and Design of Terrassa. Later, she became interested in jewellery and decided to try it in a small studio. After being fascinated by this craft, in 2011, she decided to enrol in The Llotja School of Barcelona, a school of higher education in Art and Design, to study Artistic Jewellery. Ever since, she has increased her knowledge by doing workshops in the field of jewellery and other specialities. She is currently participating in a ceramics workshop to expand her knowledge and discover new jewellery possibilities.

Martina Obid Mlakar — SWITZERLAND

/ info@martinaobid.com
/ www.martinaobid.com

The work of designer and restorer Martina Obid Mlakar is a gold- and silversmithing craft interlaced with modern materials, technologies, and needs. It is seeking answers about the role and meaning of jewellery—who or what could wear a piece of jewellery and how. The design is a successful dialog between material, shape, and story. She also pursues her interest in sculpture, graphics, and video. She has held several solo exhibitions and participated in many others, in Slovenia and abroad. Her work was accepted into the collection of the Museum of Architecture and Design Slovenia. Her works have been selected and published in books and received praise from international juries.

Mengnan Zi — CHINA

/ Mengnanzi1031@gmail.com
/ https://zimengnan.wordpress.com

Mengnan Zi is a doctoral student in design at the University of Gloucestershire and teaches at Sichuan Fine Arts Institute in China. She graduated with a Master of Jewellery Design from Birmingham City University.

Her doctoral studies are focused on design education and traditional handicraft. She has published several articles on handicraft pedagogy and sustainable development. Also, her jewellery work takes embroidery as a craft and integrates it with traditional history.

Michal Oren — ISRAEL

/ michalorenjewelry@gmail.com
/ michalorenjewelry.com

Michal Oren earned her BFA in Jewellery Design from the Bezalel Academy of Art and Design, Jerusalem, followed by an MA in Art History. "My work derives from varied sources: it responds to political and social space, but also expresses the personal and the intimate. I isolate shapes and connect them, to create pieces of jewellery whose shapes are clear. Putting together the compositions is like a game whose rules I invent every time. The intimacy of the jewellery is created through a journey of contrasts: closed forms whose ends seek continuity; or open forms that seek to be quarantined; blunt and sharp; 2D and 3D; drawing and sculpture; fineness and roughness; softness and stiffness. The form is disciplined and precise, but the meaning is amorphous, like poetry."

Michele A. Friedman — USA

/ MAFDesign1@gmail.com
/ www.micheleafriedman.com

"I was born and still reside in Chicago, IL—a city I love. My love of architecture, design, travel, history, and art is expressed throughout my work. My jewelry is the result of my desire to incorporate color into my work without using stones. The color was to be from an alternative source. Through trial & error & consideration of many materials I concluded that WOOL FELT was perfect. The material is durable, pliable, possesses a rich, saturated color and a hint of texture. I manipulate felt into shapes and set them like stones into my oxidised sterling and 18k Bi-metal jewelry. This is a technique that I developed on my own to suit my needs."

Michelle Kraemer — AUSTRIA

/ info@michellekraemer.com
/ www.michellekraemer.com

"After obtaining a degree in three-dimensional design at the University of Portsmouth, England, I continued my studies in contemporary jewellery at Alchimia, Contemporary Jewellery School in Florence, Italy with Professor Manfred Bischoff and Professor Ruudt Peters. Since 2009 I have lived and worked in Vienna, Austria, as a member of Atelier STOSSIMHIMMEL, Studio for Contemporary Jewellery, and continuously take part in exhibitions and projects, abroad as well as in Austria. I find inspiration in things that we can see but are somehow unobtainable, untouchable, unreachable. I feel the need to materialise my inner landscape into my own imagined reality."

Míriam Alsina Climent — SPAIN

/ antherea@gmail.com / www.antherea.com

Miriam Alsina graduated in Fine Arts from the University of Barcelona, where she specialised in sculpture. At the same time, inspired to create small-format sculptural pieces that function in dialogue with the female body, she studied artistic jewellery making at the Escola d'Art del Treball and the Massana School in Barcelona. Her interest in different techniques and languages moves her work in several directions. On the one hand, many of her collections feature organic shapes and sandy textures, always in black or white; while on the other she also creates lighter, more minimal pieces that play with basic geometric forms. She is also known for her work with Japanese urushi lacquer. She currently exhibits, designs, and creates jewellery at her laboratory-workshop in Barcelona.

Misato Seki — JAPAN

/ sekimisato.info@gmail.com
/ www.misatoseki.com

Misato Seki is Japanese jeweller who graduated from Tokyo National University of the Arts in 2010 with an MFA in the Department of Craft (Urushi-Art course). After completing college, she was based in Berlin and travelled around Europe to learn about contemporary jewellery. Her artwork is unique in that she utilises the constancy of Urushi and traditional decorative techniques such as Maki-e and Raden to express the beauty of the moment in ordinary, everyday life. She has taken part in many contemporary jewellery exhibitions in Japan and Germany, received the Herbert-Hofmann-Prize at Schmuck 2019, and was selected for Schmuck 2021.

Monica Krexa — ARGENTINA
/ monicakrexa@gmail.com
/ www.monicakrexa.com

"Jewellery attracted me as far back as I can remember... already as a child I recall making bracelets and necklaces out of all sorts of materials. When I was 17, I created my first aluminium collection. From there, I took different jewellery making classes and began to connect with materials such as silver and alpaca. Still, I never thought it would be more than a hobby, which is why at the same time I studied law at UBA and earned a degree. I never abandoned my true passion, and jewellery became my hobby and my sustenance. In 2002 I settled in Brazil, where 'Monica Krexa, arte en aluminio' was born. In my collections I combine commercial pieces with unique pieces. Creating with my hands is what I love to do."

Munay Martínez — ARGENTINA
/ munaymartinez@gmail.com
/ @munymartinez

Textile and clothing designer with a degree from the University of Palermo. She works and lives in Buenos Aires. She has studied jewellery since 2017 in Taller Eloi, organized by Jimena Rios. As part of her training, she participated in different workshops: "Findings" led by Manon Van Kouswijk, "The back side of the story" led by Daniela Malev; "Electroforming" led by Gaston Rois, among others. In 2019 she did a tutorial with Rodrigo Acosta. She also participated in an intensive programme led by Anastasia Young at Central Saint Martins and a workshop and exchange with the University of Cranbrook, organized by Iris Eichenberg and Jimena Rios.

Namkyung Lee — REPUBLIC OF KOREA
/ nkjewelrystudio@gmail.com
/ www.nkjewellerystudio.com

"I majored in jewellery design at Kookmin University's Graduate School of Design and am currently working in Seoul, South Korea. I have participated as a Selected Artist in various domestic and international fairs and exhibitions. I have won several awards in competitions held in Europe, such as in Spain and Italy. My works are currently in the collections of galleries in several countries.
My work takes words such as memory, image, place, and space, and shapes the concepts contained within them into abstract forms."

Natalie Hoogeveen — THE NETHERLANDS
/ info@nataliehoogeveen.nl
/ www.nataliehoogeveen.nl

Natalie Hoogeveen (1983) has been an independent goldsmith since 2005, working from her studio based in Huizen, Holland. Natalie Hoogeveen's jewels are inspired by existing and personal stories, which she transforms into unique and handmade jewellery. Aesthetic, playful, lively, colourful, and often with a humorous twist. Natalie works with silver and gold and often adds materials such as precious stones, enamel, found objects and natural products. Series vary in theme from typical Dutch characteristics, to travel themed collections and exclusive memory related pieces.

Nicole Schuster — GERMANY
/ info@nicoleschuster.com
/ www.nicoleschuster.com

Nicole Schuster is a trained goldsmith (state college for Glass & Jewellery, Kaufbeuren-Neugablonz) and designer of jewellery and objects (diploma from Pforzheim University). After a few years working in Cork, Ireland, she now has her own studio and store in Munich. Her work is shown in international exhibitions and galleries. In 2018 and 2022 she curated exhibitions showing a comparison of Japanese and German arts and crafts in jewellery and objects, presented in Tokyo (het Labo atrium) and Munich (Bavarian Arts & Crafts Council). In Nicole Schuster's work both deliberate formations and the inherent flow of nature are utilized to render symbiotic landscapes. Organic elements sprouting from lifeless shapes and constructions are often found in her pieces; this interaction is the core of the artist's creative drive.

Nóra Tengely — HUNGARY
/ tengelynora@gmail.com
/ https://tengelynora.weebly.com

"What would it be like if we chose jewellery in accordance not with sight but other senses?
We communicate via photos. We live on Instagram, Pinterest, Facebook, etc. We spend only a few seconds on an object that has been made for weeks or months. Nowadays we have less and less real physical contact with objects. As a jewellery designer, that presented me with a relevant dilemma: what is the meaning of unique jewellery design in 2017? My masterwork represents a collection of experimental jewellery, which uses the lack of visuality (every piece is monochrome) to increase tactility and create experiences. The name of the pieces came from the feelings that they cause in the wearer. My aim was to liberate associations and expand the interpretive schemes of jewellery."

Oles Tsura — GERMANY
/ o.tsura@web.de / @tsura_art

After graduating from the School of Applied and Decorative Arts in Kosiv, he entered the Lviv National Academy of Arts, where from 2012 to 2014 he studied jewellery. In 2017, he decided to pursue a degree in contemporary jewellery arts (Trier University of Applied Sciences, Faculty of Arts and Design, Idar-Oberstein Campus), graduating in January 2021 (Bachelor of Fine Arts). Currently he lives and works in Idar-Oberstein.
"Experimental ideas with natural materials always inspire me and encouraged me to create something new. My jewellery and objects are created from different materials and shapes, so that people want to touch and feel them."

Olga Košica and Rok Mar — OfR — SLOVENIA
/ olgafacesrok@gmail.com
/ ofrjewelry.com

Jewellery designer Olga Košica and graphic designer Rok Mar are the creative pair behind the Slovenian-based jewellery label OfR. Influenced by contemporary art, sculpture, painting and nature, their work is often created by combining materials, techniques and 3D printing. OfR got the public's attention when their Winter Garden and Lucid Dream collections were picked by Masha Ma to be shown at Paris Fashion Week. Since then, their work has been showcased in numerous exhibitions at home and abroad.

Olivia Shih — USA
/ olivia@oliviashih.com
/ www.oliviashih.com

Olivia Shih is a jewellery artist, designer, lapidarist, and writer based in Oakland, California. Born in the USA and raised on the subtropical island of Taiwan, she is interested in exploring human emotions and the inner life of introverts through jewellery. She holds writing and jewellery degrees from Columbia University and the California College of the Arts, respectively. Her work has been exhibited internationally, in countries such as Japan, Malaysia, Taiwan, Canada, and the USA. In addition to running her eponymous jewellery business, Olivia also writes for *Metalsmith* magazine and *Art Jewelry Forum*.

P

Patricia Mogni — ARGENTINA
/ patriciamogni@yahoo.com.ar
/ @patriciamogni
"I play and as the piece takes shape, I let it weave its own story. I'm attracted to many materials, but I give in to the humblest, to those that would be discarded. I'd like to hear it calling us and asking: what do you give value to?
I like volume, visible shapes, massive but light. A constant challenge in my work is to balance these complementary opposites. Heavy but airy, enormous but subtle.
These jewels trigger a reaction. When you see them, you can be bewildered, bemused, scornful... but you'll not be indifferent."

Paul Wells — UK
/ www.scorefoldpress.com
Paul Wells is a UK-based silversmith and jeweller, and has been teaching direct metalworking techniques for two decades. Within his practice, Wells makes innovative use of fold-forming and has developed a method of creating curved scores which can be used to fold sheet metal in a visually stunning and unique style. His pieces are intrinsically organic silver forms which almost appear to have grown themselves into existence, creating confounding biomorphic designs that are both functional and decorative. Wells' curved-score folding technique has been recognised by Goldsmiths' Crafts and Design Council with two Gold Awards for Technological Innovation. He studied at Central Saint Martins College in London.

Paula Estrada Matyášová — COLOMBIA
/ estradapaula@hotmail.com
/ www.paulaestradamatyasova.com
"I'm an industrial designer for furniture and the fashion industry. Searching for a field and a world where I could create, imagine, and communicate everything I ever wanted, I got into the jewellery world... Besides adorning the body, for me jewellery constitutes a communicating act... that holds a memory and connects the soul to the world... Regarding jewellery, I see it as a perfect three-dimensional field, multidisciplinary and apt to bond different worlds, views; aesthetic, constructing objects, design methods, concepts, and the intimate act of communicating... Objects perceived as jewels... or jewels seen as objects... The order doesn't matter... in the end, it doesn't matter, it's the result: objects and pieces with their own soul, with ALMAPROPIA. What I am looking to communicate with my work: CONNECT THE SOUL TO THE WORLD."

Petra Class — GERMANY
/ studio@petraclassjewelry.com
/ https://petraclassdesign.com
After immigrating from Germany, Petra Class, a classically trained goldsmith, founded a small jewellery design studio in San Francisco. Since then, it has grown into an atelier where a small team of gifted metalsmiths create an ever-growing collection of sculptural, contemporary jewellery. High-karat gold and gemstones are fabricated into wearable works of art.

Philip Sajet — THE NETHERLANDS
/ philipsajet@gmail.com
/ www.philipsajet.com
Philip Sajet is a thoroughbred jewellery designer. He makes jewellery for the sake of jewellery, and cannot be accused of straying into other design fields or art forms. His sectarian approach is his strength. About "B-52" Earrings: The B-52 is an airplane which flies at a height of 3 to 5 km. Impossible to see from the ground, it drops bombs. So out of the blue there are explosions. The maximum of fear and destruction in the most cowardly way imaginable.

R

Rachel Quinn — USA
/ rachel@rachelquinn.com
/ www.rachelquinn.com
Rachel Quinn is an artist and goldsmith making whimsically creative jewellery in her downtown Los Angeles studio. She draws inspiration from playful themes as well as the deeply poetic realm of the heart creating well-crafted pieces that embody romantic surrealist motifs. Rachel knew from an early age her path would be an artistic one. After receiving her BFA in painting and sculpture, Rachel moved to New York City and was soon introduced to the intoxicating world of contemporary jewellery. This introduction, by way of working for a Brooklyn jewellery artist, was the impetus to becoming a classically-trained jeweller, and in 2009 she graduated from the Metalsmith Program at The Fashion Institute of Technology. Now with over 13 years of experience, Rachel continues to hone and evolve her work as she creates delightfully unique and enduring pieces of wearable art for the expressive individual.

Ralph Bakker — GERMANY
/ ralph@luna.nl / www.ralphbakker.nl
Lives and works in Rotterdam. Works with Galerie Rob Koudijs in The Netherlands and Ornamentum Gallery in the US. Participated in numerous group exhibitions. Works in several private and public collections. "Bakker manages to unite the traditional values of refined craftsmanship with radical modernity. In his pieces he unites the Baroque with Minimalism. The key lies in the term 'unite'."

Rike Bartels — GERMANY
/ rike@rikebartels.com / www.rikebartels.com
Rike Bartels is characterised by colourful works that have a special tenderness and often humour. Born in Munich, she trained at the Massana School in Spain, then in the Black Forest, Germany, and finally in Italy, with Manfred Bischoff, whom she considers a great resource of her thinking. Last year she edited an extended monography for him.
Her work has been exhibited throughout Europe and the United States, at Museum Villa Stuck in Munich, Museum of Applied Arts in Prague, the Isabella Hund Gallery in Munich, Art Basel Design Miami Beach, Slavik Gallery in Vienna, Tefaf Maastricht, and Sotheby's in London. Publications include Art Meets Jewellery/ Gallery Slavik, New Rings, New Earrings, Danner Preis 2017, Galerie Isabella Hund/ Schmuck, and Masters: Gold.

Rita Soto Ventura — CHILE
/ rita.soto@gmail.com / www.ritasoto.cl
Artist, designer and jeweller, heir to my father's traditional jewellery craft and to centuries-old basket weaving techniques in natural fibres, with this background I have perfected the technique of micro basketry, which has been key to my artistic exploration, learning the textile language and creating jewellery that has been acclaimed and recognised in diverse fields of art, crafts, and design. "Series arise from the search for my own language and experimenting with textile, creating designs involving textile bodies and wefts, creating biomorphic objects, textile creatures that dialogue between the organic and the poetic, interweaving imaginary worlds, transforming these objects into pieces of art jewellery".

Robert Thomas Mullen — USA
/ robertthomasmullen@gmail.com
/ www.robertthomasmullen.com
Maintains a studio in St. Louis, MO. Teaches at Craft Alliance. Represented by Metal Museum, Houston Center for Contemporary Craft, Penland Gallery, Union Studio, Craft Alliance, Lux Center for the Arts and In Tandem Gallery. Received MFA in metalsmithing from Edinboro University of Pennsylvania. Been exhibited nationally and internationally.

"My materials for pieces have been collected and curated over the span of a lifetime spent waiting for the perfect piece. As I grow older and the world becomes increasingly more complicated, I look to create beautiful and simple forms. In a world of sensory overload and social media, I encourage myself to always give a quiet moment to sit and reflect. A moment to focus on the overlooked."

Roc Majoral & Enric Majoral - Majoral — SPAIN
/ info@majoral.com / www.majoral.com

Majoral is an exuberant and creative project that began on the island of Formentera in the 1970s. In touch with the values and liberating spirit of that decade, Majoral finds in arts and crafts a tool to connect with the primeval, a return to the legacy of Mediterranean cultures and a coherent and sincere way of life. Enric and Roc Majoral use their own studio-developed techniques as an expressive medium. From this experience emerge art objects that become jewellery on the skin. The strong connection with nature, source of inspiration and the backbone of Majoral's creative imagination, also leads us to an awareness of the responsibility we have regarding our environment. Since 2014 we have used guaranteed traceability metals and stones, searching for better ways to make jewellery and contribute to people's well-being.

S

Sam Woehrmann — USA
/ samwoehrmann@gmail.com
/ www.iamthatsam.com

"I've studied metal arts and gemmology with a multitude of instructors and artists from around the world, picking up knowledge and elements I put into my work from each unique experience. Finding gemstones with unique cuts and incorporating those with complementing or contrasting colors is what keeps me inspired. My work is hand fabricated and the connection between tools and materials I experience while manipulating metal gives me a grounded feeling. I like to honor the gemstones by keeping my metal work clean and minimal to let the gems speak for themselves."

Sandra Enterline — GERMANY
/ sandra@sandraenterline.com
/ www.sandraenterline.com

"My interest is in the seduction, power, and purity of valuable and ordinary materials, including my work incorporating diamond slices, glass shards and pure gold with industrial steel." Sandra graduated with an Associate's Degree in Jewellery and Metalsmithing from the Rochester Institute of Technology, School for American Craftsmen in 1980. She went on to earn a BFA in Metalsmithing from the Rhode Island School of Design in 1983. From 1991 to 1992, she held visiting professor and visiting artist positions at the School of the Museum of Fine Arts. Honours include two National Endowment for the Arts fellowships. Her pieces are part of collections, most notably the American Craft Museum, New York, NY; the Metropolitan Museum of Art, New York, NY; the Museum of Fine Arts, Boston, MA; the Renwick Gallery, National Museum of American Art at the Smithsonian Institution, Washington, D.C.; The State Hermitage Museum, St. Petersburg, Russia; and the Victoria & Albert Museum's Seymour Rabinovich Collection, London, UK.

Sandra Llusà — SPAIN
/ sandra@sandrallusa.com
/ www.sandrallusa.com

Sandra Llusà studied art and design at the Massana School in Barcelona, specializing in sculpture before pursuing a degree in jewellery arts at the same institution. Sandra is passionate about nature and tries to capture the beauty of the silence it transmits to her and transform it into jewellery. Her jewellery is delicately handmade with an abundance of patience and

time, pieces that are meticulously created so that they last a lifetime, values which she defends daily.

"Behind each piece of jewellery is a fleeting moment, almost imperceptible, that I wanted to salvage and transform into something new. A spark of light that stops me along the way, one of those moments when we catch our breath in this frenetic world that we live in."

Sandra Roldán – SRsandraroldan — COLOMBIA
/ srsandraroldan@gmail.com
/ www.srsandraroldan.com

"My academic training is as an Industrial Designer, with experience in the textile sector, specifically in fashion design. Ten years ago, I undertook a creative project called 'SRsandraroldan'. It involves the design and elaboration of personal use and/or art pieces made with thread through embroidery techniques such as crochet, macramé, and tatting, which I combine with natural stones, seeds, glass, and gold and silver thread filigree. My goal has been to create objects that, while embracing existing techniques such as the ones mentioned above, have a new use. Each of my creations is 100% handmade, filled with symbolism, and represents the culture and idiosyncrasy of at least four Colombian departments."

Sarah Al Manea — IRAQ
/ sarahalaa@azzafahmy.com

Sarah Al Manea is a designer from Iraq. She completed a two-year academic program at the design studio by Azza Fahmy. Her work must follow a concept or story she wants to tell or a cause she wants to support. She works with silver, gold, brass and courage to try different materials, to produce statement pieces. She is currently working as a teacher.

Sari Räthel & Ricarda Wolf – Räthel & Wolf — GERMANY
/ mail@rathelwolf.com / www.rathelwolf.com

"We are RÄTHEL & WOLF—a design duo celebrating the body through jewellery. Our collections are made to elevate the way one feels, contouring the silhouette with sleek and bold designs. Piercing-free and inclusive, the jewellery is handcrafted in Germany with recycled materials. Whilst sensuality is at the core of our brand, we blend digital and material cultures. With the launch of R&W Digital we have just sent out an open-ended invitation to the world to collaborate with us. By providing our designs for free to download, we offer the possibility for anyone to interact with our pieces, style their metaverse avatars, game characters or create art works with them."

Saskia Besiakov — DENMARK
/ contact@saskiabesiakov.com
/ www.saskiabesiakov.com

Saskia Besiakov received her journeyman's certificate in 2014, and was honoured with a medal from the Queen of Denmark for good craftsmanship. She opened her own workshop and boutique in 2016.
The concept of her jewellery constitutes a graphic, architectural and musical triad, in dialogue, and with the dichotomy of balance/imbalance. Hence many of the pieces appear as small harmonies, which may contain a little disharmony as a contrast. The expression must not be too "serious"; they should have some edge, playfulness, and whimsicality about them.

Selma Leal — BRAZIL
/ selmalealselmaleal@gmail.com
/ @selmalealbcn

"The Lady Musgrave collection was born because of my concerns about the collapse of the marine environment due to rising water temperatures, pollution, overfishing, etc. Especially in coral reefs, where its high biodiversity includes species among the most vulnerable or in danger of extinction, many of which are endemic to the reef system. In my work I express my love and wish for the system's speedy recovery."

Şenay Akın Durmaz — BULGARIA

/ senay@senayakin.com
/ www.senayakin.com

Şenay Akın Durmaz studied Photography at the Mimar Sinan Fine Arts University in Istanbul, followed by Jewellery Design and Gemmology courses at the Scuola d'Arte e Mestieri di Vicenza, Italy. She founded her atelier in 2008. "I love using precious materials like gold, silver, and gemstones. They are the perfect vocabulary that allows me to narrate about my secret realm of enchanted creatures. I used to travel to it in my childhood. A place where gemstones would shine in beautiful colours and fairies would dance in joy. Over time, the entrance to this realm became barely perceptible to me. Yet the feeling of it remained alive."

Silvia Bellia — GERMANY

/ silviabeemaker@gmail.com

Silvia Bellia is an Italian artist based in Germany. Her passion for engraving gemstones began in Rome, where the maestro Marcello Ripa taught her the art of glyptic. When she moved to Germany, thanks to the training by master carver Hans Ulrich Pauly, she improved her technical skills in three-dimensional carvings and worked on a wide variety of large- and smallscale gemstones. She recently completed a Master's in jewellery and gemstones at the Trier University of Applied Sciences, Idar-Oberstein Campus. Her work reflects her interest in one essential aspect of human nature, technological extension. She combines the use of new technologies, such as 3D modelling and printing, with the ancient art of stone carving.

Sofia Bankeström — SWEDEN

/ www.sofiabankestrom.com

"I hold an MFA Degree from HDK-Valand/University of Gothenburg from 2017 and have since exhibited my work nationally and internationally. I also have a background in art history and visual studies. In addition to making, an important part of my practice is teaching drawing. I find inspiration in the learning process with others, in motivating students and getting to share their progress. My work revolves around the relationship between time, materiality, and space, often referencing memory in a both personal and universal sense. By carving wood, removing material, I am looking for something that may be the essence of a material or shape. I work intuitively with different types of wood, consciously going with and against the grain."

Sofia Beilharz — GERMANY

/ info@sofiabeilharz.de / www.sofiabeilharz.de

Sofia Beilharz graduated with a BA and MA of Applied Art and Design from Hochschule Düsseldorf in Germany. She is the winner of an ART AURE award and her works have been presented at various exhibitions all over. "I am a jewellery designer living and working in Düsseldorf. My designs often revolve around geometry: spheres, circles and lines are the shapes I prefer working with the most. The jewellery becomes functional through additions of holes, cuts, curvature, and folds. Additionally, it makes the pieces appear more perceivable. Editing their surfaces causes optical effects like light reflections and shadows, which makes the pieces special and seem alive."

Sofia Jaramillo - Bocanegra — COLOMBIA

/ sofia@bocanegra.com.co / https://bocanegra.com.co

"My search has always been music. Finding something that allows me to listen to music as much as possible. One day, after finally graduating with a degree after my fifth try, I discovered this material and this technique through my mother. I began

to explore with colours and geometric shapes that connected with the questions that I took from my conversations with my creativity and my subconscious. Bocanegra is a pirate enamoured with the world and life who wanders the globe searching for the meaning of love, femininity, and vanity. She travels the seas of the unconscious to bring back the treasures she finds on her adventures and share them. Elements that ornament the body, in a new, unique, modern, and cutting-edge way."

Sogand Nobahar — IRAN

/ info@nobahardesign.com / www.nobahardesign.com

Nobahar Design Milano tells the story of traditional and modern values coming together from living in Italy and Iran. It combines my background in art, my education in Industrial and Jewellery Design, as well as Engineering. Nobahar Design Milano was founded in 2017 to express the experiences of a life lived in this chaotic world. The kind of world that stops us from going beyond the ordinary. The kind of world that emphasises sticking to conventional ways of living. Nobahar Design Milano explores this world to learn and experience more of life. Some say it is unconventional. However, that is Nobahar Design's way of connecting and inspiring people to live life to the fullest.

Stefan Gougherty — USA

/ info@stefangougherty.com
/ www.stefangougherty.com

Drawing upon his technical design background, Stefan Gougherty creates jewellery that is both a celebration and critique of human ingenuity. His previous career—designing wearable technology for Google—informs his metalsmithing process: practicality, manufacturability and industrial processes are leveraged to create unusual, yet highly functional objects. Fascinated by the interactive potential of jewellery, Stefan integrates sound, kinetics and other interactive features that become activated through wearing. With content mined from opposing forces such as trash/treasure, ancient/future and public/private, his work mirrors the paradox (and humour) of this strange world we inhabit.

Stefania Lucchetta — ITALY

/ www.stefanialucchetta.com

Stefania holds a BA with Honours in Literature and Art History from Ca' Foscari University of Venice and a MA from the Scuola Italiana Design of Padua. After training as a goldsmith in her family business, she began to focus on 3D software and rapid prototyping machines in 1999. In 2002, Stefania started producing her one-of-a-kind jewels, exploring experimental techniques and materials while still working as an industrial designer. She is considered a pioneer of additive technologies applied to several materials such as stellite and titanium to create an innovative language for jewellery.

Thanks to her innovative research, she has been invited to give lectures at Politecnico di Milano, and her works have been exhibited in important museums worldwide.

Stefanie Verhoef — THE NETHERLANDS

/ info@stefanieverhoef.com
/ www.stefanieverhoef.com

I completed a technical goldsmith degree in Amsterdam and hold a Bachelor's degree in Fine Arts and Education. Throughout my art studies, jewellery and design have always played a big role. For several years I have taught goldsmithing techniques, and now I work fulltime as a designer and maker.

Being trained as a goldsmith, a fine arts artist, and an art teacher, I've learned many ways of creating and expressing. Designing and making jewellery is the core and working within the contemporary and conceptual field is where I feel most comfortable. For me the experience of art is very much a matter of feeling and understanding in your own personal and private way. I think of creating art as the greatest personal and private act. Like wearing jewellery.

Stephanie Jendis — GERMANY

"Stones are where my work starts. I use natural stones, as well as crystalline and stone shapes, which I make from other materials like wood or plastic. My work consists of sorting and grouping—I arrange and re-arrange, create regularities, disorder, and exceptions… Precious stones always possess a sense of glamour and secrecy… My jewellery is colourful but not brightly coloured. Differences in colours and materials produce moods, which I have sought to capture."

Stephie Morawetz — AUSTRIA
/ stephie.morawetz@gmail.com
/ stephiemorawetz.com

Stephie Morawetz is an artist from Austria. Stephie graduated with a Bachelor of Arts in millinery (hat-making) from the University Linz. Furthermore, she successfully completed her Bachelor of Fine Arts studies in Idar-Oberstein, Germany. She did her master studies at Shenkar College of Engineering, Design and Art in Tel Aviv, Israel. In 2017 she founded, together with Laura Jack, the non-profit organization NOD – Not Only Decoration, for social and environmental jewellery.

Susanne Henry — USA
/ sghenry@aol.com

Susanne Henry creates jewellery in an evolving exploration of chain-making and its elements. She explores scale, movement and flow, structure and form, and steel and gold. Susanne is an American jewellery artist and metalsmith in Chicago. In recent years, she has been in juried and curated group shows, including MAD About Jewelry at the Museum of Arts and Design in New York in 2021. She was also featured in the article on Next Career Artists, "Coming of Age", in *Metalsmith* magazine in 2020. Susanne graduated from the Rhode Island School of Design with a BFA in Industrial Design. After an MBA and a multi-faceted career in business, she learned metalsmithing at Lillstreet Art Center, and is a self-taught artist.

Tala Yuan — CHINA
/ yntala@126.com

Tala Yuan was born in Jieyang, Province Guandong, P.R. China. BA in Product Design, South China Normal University, Guangzhou, P.R. China; BA and MFA in Gemstone and Jewellery, University of Applied Sciences Trier / Idar-Oberstein, Germany. She currently works as head of the jewellery design and craft department in Shenzhen Polytechnic. She lives in Shenzhen.

Tass Joies — SPAIN
/ tass@tassjoies.com / tassjoies.com

Tass Joies is a handcrafted jewellery company in Barcelona with 27 years of experience. Managed and staffed by women, we base our collections on designs inspired by nature and our immediate surroundings. Sustainability, empathy, recycling… These are values that move us to improve the natural and social environment. All the designs are made by hand, from the initial sketches to the final touches, always searching for excellence in what we do. We design innovative author collections, jewellery that is agile and fresh, always appropriate whatever the occasion. We create jewellery with soul.

Teresa Milheiro — PORTUGAL
/ teresamilheiroarticula@gmail.com
/ www.teresamilheiro.com

With an artistic academic background from the António Arroio Art School, IADE and AR.CO, together with a career in art production of more than thirty years, in 1994 she co-founded the Zé dos Bois Gallery. From 1998 and for 10 years, she collaborated with the company Archeofactu working on jewellery collections aimed at institutions and museums, inspired by their material heritage, maintaining, at the same time, her own individual and independent creation and production. In 2007 she opened the Articula Gallery. Her work can be found in MUDE- Museum of Fashion and Design; in national and international collections; and in several national and international catalogues and publications. She has participated in conferences and debates, and was also a judge in several contests. She taught jewellery at Ar.Co. from 2016 to 2019.

Terhi Tolvanen — FINLAND
/ www.terhitolvanen.com

Terhi Tolvanen is Finnish jewellery artist working and living in France. She finished her art studies in Amsterdam in 1999 and has been making and exhibiting studio jewellery ever since. In her work she visualises the relationship between man and nature. Terhi is fascinated especially by human interference in nature; the traces that are left behind by taking care, organizing or controlling nature. For her, nature is all about light, colour and rhythms in its organization and construction. Her work contemplates the dialogue between these different elements.

Theresa De Jager – Pistol & Peach — SOUTH AFRICA
/ info@pistolandpeach.com
/ www.pistolandpeach.com

Born and raised in South Africa. Theresa completed her Jewellery Design degree at CPUT in Cape Town. She finished her Masters in 2012 at NCAD in Dublin, Ireland where she specialised in ideas of "Investigations into the preciousness of digital jewellery design." The project concentrated around the integration of rapid prototyping technology into a jewellery designer's practice. Post study, Theresa started a small jewellery practice and studio with her partner, 'Pistol and Peach' in 2013 in Cape Town, and they subsequently relocated to the United Kingdom in 2016. Their studio regularly produces work for showcases, galleries and independent stockists throughout the UK and Ireland.

Tobias Andersson — SWEDEN
/ toberik.ta@gmail.com
/ @tobias.a.jewelleryart

"I have contributed with the earring Pearl that refers to the picture called *Girl with the Pearl Earring* (c. 1665) by Johannes Vermeer.
During the last 21 years I have mostly been working with the existential vanitas or *memento mori* theme. The human skull has always been there, a timeless and classical form that all humans can relate to.
The skull has come to be my canvas for enamelling oxidation, etc. which I 'paint' and burn directly with a torch. I work in quite a raw and expressive way."

Uli Biskup Schmuck — GERMANY
/ louisasophieb@web.de
/ www.ulibiskup.de

After her goldsmith apprenticeship and diploma in product and jewellery design, Uli Biskup worked as a self-employed jewellery designer and co-owned workshop galleries. Recently, she has mostly participated in international exhibitions and fairs. Uli'ss work in general is rather reduced and seemingly "simple", often delicate and light. She is looking for considerate and thoughtful ways to deal with materials and their specific qualities. Precise manufacturing and a pleasant wearability are likewise important for her idea of good jewellery.
Earrings are some of her favourite pieces of jewellery to make. What fascinates her about them are their lightweight structures and flattering movements.

Ute Decker — GERMANY
/ ud@utedecker.com / www.utedecker.com
Described as "the architectural jeweller," the wearable sculptures of Ute Decker are a meditation on the richness of simplicity. In her one-off and limited-edition pieces she sculpts space, movement, and volume into a carefully composed interplay of light and shadow, movement, and serenity. With a degree in Political Economics and a background in journalism, Decker is a leading pioneer of the ethical jewellery movement. Working in Fairtrade Gold and recycled silver, her pieces are exhibited internationally and held in several public collections including the Victoria and Albert Museum, London.

Ute Eitzenhöfer — GERMANY
Ute Eitzenhöfer was trained as a goldsmith in Pforzheim and Karlsruhe and graduated from Pforzheim University in 1996 with a diploma in jewellery and tableware. She has been a freelancer since 1996 and in 2005 was appointed professor of gemstone design at Trier University of Applied Sciences, Faculty of Art and Design, Department of Gemstones and Jewellery at the Idar-Oberstein campus. Her works are exhibited internationally in museums and galleries and are in public and private collections.

V

Valentina Falchi — SPAIN
/ info@valentinafalchi.com / valentinafalchi.com
"For me jewellery is not, and should not be, a symbol of luxury but an element that recognizes the personality and spirit of the person wearing it. Jewellery, pure art, is feeling!" These words from designer Valentina Falchi describe her vision of jewellery. Her designs are notable for lines and textures, both geometric and organic, filled with details inspired by daily life, nature and sensations, which Valentina expresses in a modern style with a strong identity. In 2007, after completing her studies in Florence, she began her career as a designer in Barcelona, where she has her own studio. Since 2015 she has been the coordinator and professor of jewellery design studies at IED Barcelona.

Valeria D'Annibale – Varily Jewellery — ITALY
/ info@varilyjewelry.com
Valeria is an Italian contemporary jewellery designer and maker based in The Hague. Born and raised in Italy, Valeria moved to Sydney, Australia, where she started her jewellery brand. She studied goldsmithing in Rome and Jewellery & Object Design in Sydney. The 3D printing process allows Valeria to create pieces in a controlled and precise way, still being able to add a handmade element while maintaining the object's geometric perfection. Printed nylon has a great influence on Valeria's practice, allowing her to experiment with material possibilities and push the boundaries of what is possible.

Vania Ruiz – CasaKiro — CHILE
/ contacto@casakiro.cl / www.casakiro.cl
"As architect by trade, I've always felt the need to work with my hands. Jewellery awarded me the opportunity to combine the things that have fascinated me since I was a little girl: painting, creating, and telling stories. Through my brand Casa Kiro, I've been able to live a creative, happy, and intense life for 12 years, making original and artistic pieces of jewellery that bestow joy, beauty, and power on those who wear them. Jewellery that makes the wearer stand out, because life is too short to be discreet. 'The Mariposas' (Butterfly) collection emerged timidly in 2019, and flourished during the pandemic, including today an extensive variety of species from across the world. The pieces are painted by hand on epoxy resin and silver fittings in a handcrafted and laborious process that I carry out with three other women."

Vika Mayzel — ISRAEL
/ info@vikamayzel.com / www.vikamayzel.com
Vika Mayzel is an Israeli jewellery designer. In 2015 she graduated from the Jewellery Design Department of Shenkar College of Engineering and Design, in Ramat Gan, Israel, with a bachelor's degree in design. Currently she lives and works in Prague, Czech Republic.
Vika devoted over 10 years to fine and pictorial art, and her jewellery is linked to an artistic foundation in details, search of new forms and smoothness of lines. This dialogue between jewellery and the world of art is ongoing. She creates contemporary jewellery pieces, finding a perfect balance between ever trendy minimalism and tribal aesthetics, between bold geometry and a traditional amulet.

Violeta Adomaitytė — LITHUANIA
/ adomaityte.violeta@gmail.com
/ www.violetaadomaityte.it
"At age 19 I went to the Vilnius Academy of Arts to study printmaking. It was the beginning of working with metal (etching plates) and the beginning of working with stone (lithography). This fascination with metal and stone has never stopped; from there to making jewellery was just a small step. I see printmaking as a depiction of a reality, but what I do is create reality itself. Then you can touch it. It is real. Jewellery is magic."

Vivian S.Q. Shi — CHINA
/ siqi.zhu@network.rca.ac.uk
/ siqijewelry.com
Vivian S.Q., maker, and conceptual artist, holds a Bachelor of Engineering degree from Donghua University and studied Jewellery and Metal in an MA course at the Royal College of Art. She aims to explore the role of contemporary jewellery in spreading socially hot issues. Most of her projects are about socially hot topics (environmental issues, consumerism issues) or vulnerable groups. She hopes that these works can arouse the public's attention rather than be forgotten.

W

Wesley Zwiep — THE NETHERLANDS
/ wzwiep@hotmail.com / www.zwiep.co.uk
Wesley grew up in the Netherlands and was encouraged to be creative from an early age. After beginning his working life in the world of fashion he moved to Scotland in 2008. Following his training as a goldsmith and stone-setter, Wesley became a director at ORRO Contemporary Jewellery gallery in Glasgow. Utilising traditional skills hand in hand with CAD drawing and 3D printing he has developed his own unique style. Wesley's pieces always have form following function as a prime motivation. The gold rivets on his signature pieces are there as an integral part of the structure, holding it together. They add a decorative detail, but this is merely incidental as functionality is their primary purpose. "My work has elements which, in some people, evoke memories of stained-glass windows or of mediaeval art, while others contrastingly, see industrial or mechanical forms in it. I leave it up to the individual to see what they will in my work."

X

Xiao Chen — CHINA
/ chenxiao0410@yahoo.com
/ xiao-chen.com
Xiao CHEN, born in China, is working and living in France. After getting a diversified education in plastic arts in China and France, she joined AFEDAP to learn jewellery craftsmanship. She then continued her research at the Limoges art academy, where she developed a protocol allowing a symbiotic exchange between the object/jewellery and different media to give birth to hybrid works where a wearable object carries a story.
The different cultures and politics of the two countries she lived in make her question daily life. In her works, the ideas

of ambiguity, contradiction, perfection, and imperfection are important. She crafts with basic materials; her pieces get magnified by their simplicity. The objective isn't just aesthetic, but gives intelligence to those pieces.

Xiao Han Zhang — CHINA
/ 2457104585@qq.com

Undergraduate at Sichuan Fine Arts Institute, Arts and Crafts, Xiao Han Zhang won the title of "Excellent Student Cadre" in 2019-2020 and obtain the third class scholarship for excellent students in 2019-2020 academic year.

Xinia Guan — CHINA
/ www.xiniaguan.com

Xinia Guan was born and raised in Inner Mongolia, China. She has a dual B.A. degree in Literature and Economics from Inner Mongolia University. She studied for an M.F.A. in jewellery at Savannah College of Art and Design. She has had several exhibitions in the USA, Europe, and China, participated in JOYA Barcelona 2019, Munich Jewellery Week 2020, 2021, and Athens Awards of Jewellery Week 2020. Winner of PREZIOSA YOUNG 2021. BKV-Preis Young Applied Arts finalist. Excellence Prize of Japan Jewellery Competition. Her area of practice is using traditional materials through the hand sawing and hand fabrication process to approach an extreme geometric aesthetic. The combination of time and space has become everything in her current pieces.

Y

Yeena Yoon — REPUBLIC OF KOREA
/ info@yeenayoon.com / www.yeenayoon.com

Yeena Yoon studied at the world-renowned Architectural Association. She has worked for many award-winning architectural practices including KPF, AHMM and Zaha Hadid Architects. Inspired by Zaha Hadid's exploration of design, and how she channelled her creativity into multiple projects, including furniture, fashion, and jewellery, Yeena decided to explore ways to express her own creativity. Discovering jewellery making, Yeena studied at the highly respected Goldsmiths' Centre Setting Out programme as well as learning under mastercraftsmenGiovanni Corvaja and Charlotte De Syllas, receiving the Queen Elizabeth Scholarship Trust in 2021 as well as the GemX scholarship in 2022. With a powerful interest in materials, Yeena applies a philosophy of questioning the idea of what is precious, juxtaposing themes and materials to realise the full potential of Yeena Yoon fine jewellery.

Yojae Lee — REPUBLIC OF KOREA
/ leeyojae@naver.com
/ klimt02.net/jewelers/yojae-lee

"Insects are easily spotted around us but they are considered as something that people don't want to look or think about because of their different appearance. I was attracted by their different and strange proportion and colours so I wanted to express them from my point of view. The main material of my work is animal skin, and it can be visually offensive. But it gives infinite inspiration and powerful force as the material enables me to make various attempts. It brings interesting yet strange feelings by being combined with the uniqueness that you feel from the shape and skin of insects. These two different feelings are reproduced in something attractive by generating subtle tension. I hope viewers can share my feeling and view through my work."

Youjin Um — REPUBLIC OF KOREA
/ genei2001@hanmail.net
/ https://klimt02.net/jewellers/youjin-um

"I am a metal craft designer. I like the natural properties of cold metal materials, especially the clear and transparent colours of silver. The beginning of my work is to create drawings in advance and model them in paper to virtually grasp the real feeling. Then, after attaching drawings and leaving a mark on the silver plate, they begin to project. Through the way I pierce and express myself one by one, I feel healing, relief, and happiness in life."

Yuki Sumiya — JAPAN
/ info@yukisumiya.com / yukisumiya.com

Yuki Sumiya is a contemporary jewellery artist based in Kamakura, Japan. Sumiya graduated from Joshibi College Art and Design, Department of Metalsmithing in Tokyo, Japan in 1993. After graduating, Sumiya worked for a metalsmithing company as a blacksmith, and after that, she worked as apprentice for jewellery artist Fumiko Hoshi, serving as a goldsmith. In 2005, Sumiya moved to Florence, Italy to study under Manfred Bischiff at Alchimia Contemporary Jewellery School. After graduating Alchimia, she returned to Japan and established a jewellery studio in her home. Her work has been exhibited both in solo and group shows in galleries and fairs such as Cominelli Foundation Collections. This work is based on the motif of structures, created from the memories of a journey.

Z

Zhanna Assanova — PAKISTAN
/ assanovajeanna@gmail.com
/ @assanova.jeanna

"I am a jewellery designer from Kazakhstan, a wife of a diplomat. Because of our job we often move from one country to another, meeting different people from different countries. And I am often asked about Kazakhstan, its traditions and culture, and I always talk about our artisans, the old technique in jewellery and applied art.

I'd like to present the earrings in national Kazakh "Kurak" patchwork style. Ancient Turkic people used to make carpets in that way and these earrings are an example of the combination of traditional technique, the idea and modern material - a zip. It is an ethnicity and modern creation at the same time.

My main idea is to keep a gene (birth) thread which connects us with our ancestors, their history and culture."

Zhuyun Chen — CHINA
/ zhuyun.jewellery@gmail.com
/ www.zhuyunchen.com

Zhuyun Chen is a London-based jewellery designer and a recent graduate from Central Saint Martins. In her eyes, jewellery is not just an object but an experience. Her work explores a playful way of wearing and viewing jewellery through a unique optical illusion called the Moiré Effect. The structures overlap and create dynamic illusions, turning jewellery from a still object into an engaging experience. Each earrings reflects intricacy and delicacy through an integration of 3D printing and traditional handmade processes. Zhuyun reimagines the possibilities of optical illusions for contemporary jewellery through design, craft, and interactive experience, creating moments of surprise for both the wearer and the viewer through her jewellery.

About
the author

Nicolas Estrada

Nicolas Estrada (b. Medellín, Colombia, 1972) discovered his artistic pathway in Barcelona, a city that he had come to for entirely different reasons. Until that point, he had been an inhabitant of the business world, where he was involved in marketing. His destiny, however, was to follow another path: creating one-off jewellery artworks that were meaningful, unique and infused with stories that speak to the senses.

At Barcelona's Llotja and Massana schools, Nicolas came into contact with the world of jewellery for the first time. In this world, he discovered that his efforts opened up infinite possibilities for expression to him. He is a tireless researcher of his craft, and his curiosity and passion for this discipline have led him into many different territories along the path toward balance and perfection. He has studied widely, learning the techniques of gemmology, setting and engraving. He has also produced research and works through his involvement in, for example, the traditional Berber jewellery of Kabylia; the filigree techniques practised in the Colombian town of Santa Cruz de Mompox; and master's-level studies in gemstone carving and jewellery design at the University of Trier in Germany.

The subjects from which Nicolas takes inspiration for his pieces relate directly to the humanity and sensibility of those who view them. They are not pieces that seek to defend or take positions on central, significant situations in his country and his continent. Instead, they are the pure and clear gaze of an artist who seeks, through the tools offered by his artistic work, to provide new perspectives. For Nicolas, each piece of jewellery is imbued with immense power and value. A poetic offering of the kind contained in Nicolas's work emerges through interpreting his powerful and meaning-laden artistic reflections, conveyed by means of an intimate dialogue between the object and the gaze of the other.

Professionally, Nicolas Estrada develops the extraordinary and the provocative. His works can be found in galleries around the world from Glasgow to Riga, San Francisco or Barcelona. His pieces are handmade, personal and, transgressive. His work is a hymn to irreverence and reflection, and it is immersed in the aura of a discipline practiced with judgment and deep thought. Over the course of 2018, Nicolas gave lectures and workshops at universities and art centres in England, Germany and the United States. In Birmingham (UK), he led a workshop on visual documentation for jewellery students at Birmingham City University and gave a 'Talking Practice' lecture at the School of Jewellery. He was the 'Mainstage Speaker' at Makers Across Disciplines Engage, the 47th annual conference of the Society of North American Goldsmiths, held at Portland, Oregon in the USA. And he taught the design course 'Transforming non-traditional jewellery materials into jewellery' at the Akademie für Gestaltung und Design in Munich, Germany, attended by a group of students from the Pakistan Institute of Fashion and Design. In 2019, he was invited to represent his homeland, Colombia, at World Art Tokyo in Japan, where he also had the opportunity to give a lecture and lead a workshop at the Hiko Mizuno College of Jewellery in Tokyo, Japan's most highly regarded jewellery school.

Nicolas is the author of five books in a series on jewellery that has been published by Hoaki in several languages and distributed worldwide: *New Rings: 500+ Designs from Around the World*, an updated version of which was subsequently published by Thames & Hudson; *New Earrings: 500+ Designs from Around the World*; *New Necklaces: 400+ Designs in Contemporary Jewellery*; *New Brooches: 400+ Contemporary Jewellery Designs*; and *New Bracelets: 400+ Contemporary Jewellery Designs*, a book that showcases more than 400 bracelets by 200 jewellers, who were selected from among a pool of 900 artists hailing from all parts of the world.

After living many years in Barcelona, the city that allowed him to be who he wanted to be and to do what he wanted to do, Nicolas currently lives in Colombia.